RED CLAY
ON MY
BOOTS
Encounters with Khe Sanh
1968 to 2005

By Robert J. Topmiller

Kirk House Publishers
Minneapolis, Minnesota

Red Clay on My Boots
Encounters with Khe Sanh, 1968 to 2005
Robert J. Topmiller

Copyright 2007 Kirk House Publishers. All rights reserved. Except for brief quotations in critical articles or reviews, no part of this book may be reproduced in any manner without prior permission of the publisher.

(All photos in this book came from the author's personal collection except where other sources are noted).

Publisher's Cataloging-In-Publication Data
(Prepared by The Donohue Group, Inc.)

Topmiller, Robert J., 1948-
Red clay on my boots : encounters with Khe Sanh, 1968 to 2005 / Robert J. Topmiller.
 p. : ill. ; cm.
 ISBN-13: 978-1-933794-05-1
 ISBN-10: 1-933794-05-4
 1. Topmiller, Robert J. 2. Vietnam War, 1961-1975—Personal narratives,
American. 3. Khe Sanh, Battle of, Vietnam, 1968. I. Title.
DS557.8.K5 T66 2007
959.704/3/092

                                                        2007923826

Kirk House Publishers, PO Box 390759, Minneapolis, MN 55439
Manufactured in the United states of America

To the sick children of Vietnam

Contents

Preface

The Extraordinary Price of Warfare

In 1968, I went to Vietnam for the first time as a nineteen-year-old hospital corpsman (medic) with the 26th Marines. Today, the level of misery inflicted on U.S. forces at Khe Sanh in the early months of 1968 seems almost incomprehensible to Americans familiar with the high-tech/low-casualty conflicts of the post-Vietnam War era. Yet, according to Chaplain Ray Stubbe, a Khe Sanh battle participant, the base received 11,114 rounds of incoming rocket, artillery, and mortar fire from the beginning of the siege in January until April 1968. He estimated that some 573 Americans died defending the outpost while enemy fire wounded an additional 2,000 U.S. personnel. If one adds the close-to-500 non-battle losses during this period, the total casualty figures rise to more than 3,000—roughly half of the troops stationed there at any one time during the siege. Moreover, as Mike Archer points out in *A Patch of Ground: Khe Sanh Remembered*, over 1,000 Americans died in the Khe Sanh area alone during 1968.

Astoundingly, we incurred 3,000 dead and wounded in less than three months defending a position that the U.S. soon abandoned and the Peoples Army of Vietnam (PAVN, better known as the North Vietnamese Army or NVA during the war) seized by July 1968, within months of the end of the siege. In an extremely painful and exquisite irony, the Vietnamese assert that they won the battle of Khe Sanh despite their shocking losses and our persistent claims of victory.

My Khe Sanh experiences sparked a lifetime of profound alienation from the society around me. Indeed, I have often under-

The US Army's CH-47 air freighter on display at the Tà Cơn Airport Monument. — VNS Photo Đức Dục.

US choppers draw tourists to former Khe Sanh base

QUẢNG TRỊ — Two US helicopters now form part of the war relics' collection at the Tà Cơn Airport Monument at the former Khe Sanh Base in the central province of Quảng Trị on Tuesday.

The helicopters, an HU-1H and a CH-47 air-freighter, were used by the US Army during the American War and were handed over in celebration of the 35th Anniversary of the Khe Sanh victory (9 July 1968).

They were donated by the Ministry of Defence to the Quảng Trị Monument's Conservation Management Board for display at the Tà Cơn Airport Monument Complex.

Around 100 war artefacts, 150 documents and photographs relating to the campaign to liberate the Khe Sanh Base in the summer of 1968 are part of the collection at the monument.

The tunnels at Vĩnh Mốc and the complex are the main attractions of the DMZ (De-militarised Zone) tours in Quảng Trị.—**VNS**

Vietnamese article about PAVN victory (2003)

gone feelings of isolation, immense survivor's guilt, bitterness, revulsion, uncontrollable emotion, and remorse. But I have also been consumed with rage, an intense abiding anger that has affected the quality of my life and the existence of those around me, an often-uncontrollable fury that I seldom understood and that resided just under the surface of my consciousness.

Now, the ferocity of my rancor has turned into a dull ache, a source of unimaginable pain impossible to describe but nonetheless always lurking on the edge of my awareness. Even today, after so many years, memories of Vietnam trigger the most extreme reaction; my eyes fill with tears, my voice cracks, and I have to summon all of my self-control to avoid bursting into tears. Along with my emotional attachment to the war existed the most persistent sensation of all: a never-ending, pervasive, controlling anxiety. Indeed, for decades I have dreaded closed spaces, rats, failure, vulnerability, and having other people discover the depth of my trepidation.

I am constantly troubled by Vietnam. Perhaps I feel shame because of what we did to the Vietnamese or maybe I understand that I could have done so much more. Possibly if I had been braver or more competent more Marines would be alive today. Definitely I should have been more vocal in my opposition to the war when I returned home. Or, possibly I realize that my continued existence resulted from pure luck and that blind fate condemned those who died in my place. Whatever the reason, I find myself wracked with guilt everyday.

My efforts to come to terms with Khe Sanh compelled me to visit postwar Vietnam, because like many vets I found myself both attracted and repelled by the war. But, I shrank from the thought of going back as well. Finally, in 1996, I returned to Vietnam and Khe Sanh in what would be the first of many trips over the next decade. Those journeys helped me understand the impact of the conflict on the Vietnamese people. Nevertheless, during my first morning in Vietnam in 1996, it took every ounce of courage I could muster to walk out of my hotel after a night of fitful sleep. I wondered what I might find there: the individual I wanted to be, the person I might have been, or the being I am? Others had returned to old battle scenes and escaped their demons. Would I? Would the nightmares end? Would I be able to sleep through the night for the first time in almost thirty years? Would I be worse? Or, most horrible of all, would nothing change? Would I forever be consigned to a life ruled by fear and guilt? Would the screams of wounded men still visit me at night?

While my struggle to confront the war has been long and difficult, certainly the conflict did not affect just me. Violence exerts an immeasurable human cost that never completely departs. When I look at the Vietnam War, I see only pain, because wars never really end for those who participate in them. War comprises the most dehumanizing experience anyone can ever endure. Nothing honorable, gallant, or reaffirming results from seeing men blown to pieces. Wars create agony for those who fight them, while the anguish of battle never fades but resides forever as a deep, throbbing pain and an awareness of how truly transitory life and sanity remain. Not surprisingly, I have come to hate warfare while also realizing that only an attitude of peace, reconciliation, and forgiveness will ever allow Americans and Vietnamese to recover from the hostilities.

Several years ago, my wife introduced me to a young man at the University of Kentucky (UK). After I advised him that I had come to UK to work on a dissertation on the war, he asked me if I was a veteran. When I said yes, his eyes filled with tears and he told me the story of his father, who had returned from Vietnam with Post Traumatic Stress Disorder (PTSD), became an alcoholic and eventually died of cancer—most likely induced from Agent Orange (A/O)—a month after the Veterans Administration (VA) finally granted him a disability. While he spoke, I recognized that the war had ruined his life and his relationship with his father. What a terrible, tragic loss for anyone to suffer. His life merely echoed that of many other veterans' children. The next day, he informed my wife that as soon as he found out my veteran's status, he knew he could talk to me about his father.

When I taught my course on the Vietnam War, I often became a surrogate father for many young people who desperately wanted their fathers to recover from the conflict and connect emotionally with them. Paradoxically, many young Americans in the twenty-first century admired Vietnam vets because we "did the right thing and went to Vietnam." Did we? Of course, many looked up to me because they suspected that inside my placid, non-violent exterior lurked a Rambo-like killing machine ready to burst forth at the slightest provocation. But I was, at best, a reluctant and not particularly competent warrior. If truth be told, when I looked back at Vietnam, I only saw my failures.

While I was jogging near my home one afternoon in 1999, a woman driving by noticed my Vietnam running shirt and cut me off with her car. When she got out of her vehicle, she asked me, "Were you in that Vietnam War?" I approached her with some trepidation because discussing the conflict often unleashed powerful emotions, even after a quarter of a century. After I said yes and inquired why she wanted to know, she responded, "My brother died in Vietnam and I hope you might have known him." Unfortunately, I did not. I surmised that she must have been around ten years old when she lost her brother. In her grief and longing, she had been reduced to approaching strangers in a desperate hope that someone could connect her with a dead sibling. I spent the remainder of the run, and a long time afterward, thinking about this devastated woman who would do just about anything to get her brother back.

Several years later I spoke at an antiwar teach-in at my university when one of the speakers asked if I had ever been in Quang Tri Province (the northernmost province in the former South Vietnam). When I said yes, he began to cry and told me that his brother had been killed in Quang Tri Province in 1968. I often reflected on the pain of the families who lost loved ones in a conflict that many Americans now believe constituted a terrible mistake. How do I explain to someone that his/her child or parent or brother/sister died for nothing?

Yet, for all of the suffering Americans experienced from the conflict, the terrible times we endured and the families who grieved, nobody lost as much as did the South Vietnamese because they forfeited their freedom and their country and had lived for over three decades under a political party that hated them for fighting alongside the Americans and punished them repeatedly for it.

What a stunning absurdity I felt as I witnessed my country slip into a new, confusing struggle in Iraq that would create another generation of bitter, disillusioned vets and cynical chicken hawks. As I spilled my bitterness onto these pages, I began to comprehend how deeply the war continued to wound me, other vets, former ARVN (Army of the Republic of Vietnam, the South Vietnamese army), PAVN combatants, and the children of Vietnam. But I was just one vet trying to find his way through a minefield of erroneous assumptions amid the misguided admiration that suddenly had surrounded us. That may be better than the loser image we carried after the conflict, but neither remained very accurate. Was it just as bad to idealize us as it was to demonize us?

These experiences, and many more than I could ever relate, led me for close to forty years to try, with little success, to make sense out of the pointless sacrifices of so many Americans and Vietnamese during and after the war. Everywhere I turned, more-over, I confronted constant reminders of the shattered lives, broken hearts, ruined minds, and wrecked families brought on by the conflict. Remembering that real people and families suffered deeply because of the fighting made my quest for answers even more compelling. This book is their story as well as mine.

While it remains difficult to acknowledge adequately the many contributions made by friends and colleagues during the assembly of this work, a few stand out and deserve special recognition. Eastern Kentucky University (EKU), the Marine Corps Historical

Foundation, the Lyndon Baines Johnson Foundation, and the University of Kentucky awarded me generous grants that allowed me to make numerous research trips to Vietnam, Laos, and Cambodia. I particularly want to thank the EKU University Research Committee, the EKU Provost's office, the EKU College of Arts and Sciences and, most of all, the EKU History Department, principally its Travel Committee, for their continuous assistance for my research.

I would also like to acknowledge the authors of previous books on Khe Sanh who helped me better understand the historical dimensions of the battle: Ray Stubbe, John Prados, Mike Archer, Robert Pisor, John Corbett, Eric Hammel, and Michael Herr. In addition, I want to express my sincere thanks to the University Press of Kentucky for granting me permission to reprint some sections from my first book, *The Lotus Unleashed: The Buddhist Peace Movement in South Vietnam, 1964-1966.*

I also want to convey appreciation to my associates who assisted me in putting this project together. My good friend Tom Appleton read numerous drafts of this work and made many helpful suggestions. My research assistant Deb Boggs remained eager and ready to assist my many requests for information. My doctor at the Lexington VA hospital, Kim Larmore, provided me with lots of encouragement and always made himself available as I charted my way through this manuscript. My long-lost Khe Sanh buddies, Mike Archer and Steve Orr, also reviewed this work and gave me invaluable support and help on this project. My drinking cronies Eric Christianson, Bob Stubblefield, and son Rob remained steadfast in supplying me with beer and encouragement, as did the friendly staffs at Billy's Barbeque and Charlie Browns. The former chair of the EKU history department, Ron Huch, always managed to find me extra research money while also providing me a flexible schedule that made this book possible.

Finally, I want to express my greatest gratitude to the three women who kept me from going over the edge on many occasions: Karen Kitterman from the Kittitas County Comprehensive Mental Health Service in Ellensburg, Washington, Dr. Cynthia Dunn from the Lexington Kentucky VA hospital and, most important, my wife Terri, who has fought the battle of Khe Sanh by my side for close to forty years.

Introduction

"There is no place in this country for people like you anymore."
- Eastern Kentucky University employee

January 21, 1968

I have relived this day at least a thousand times. Every year as January 21 approaches, I become progressively apprehensive and consumed with feelings of impending doom and dread that another catastrophe like Khe Sanh might again come to pass at a different place in another era, but with the same spellbinding terror and revulsion as in 1968. I even feel the consequences of this grisly day when I teach my class on the history of the Vietnam War. As the course moves chronologically towards 1968, my angst and subsequent depression increases. But at least now I can talk about it, although I have struggled mightily to hang on to my sanity since that day close to forty years ago.

On the morning of January 21, 1968, I awoke to the sound of strange whistling noises outside my aid station at Khe Sanh, South Vietnam. I heard people yelling and running around amid increasingly loud explosions and screaming incoming rounds as I ran towards the front door to enter the small bunker in front of our medical facility. After I stepped out of the doorway, flashes of light and explosions seemed to be occurring everywhere. I hesitated, fascinated by the lethal light show taking place in front of my eyes, whereupon a chief petty officer pushed me through the door and into the dugout.

Crammed in the bunker with the rest of our medical staff, I recognized for the first time that I really could die in Vietnam. My reaction also confirmed the truism that few atheists inhabit foxholes. I prayed harder than I had in years for the Lord to deliver me from the horrors descending on us at that instant and promised good behavior and strict adherence to heavenly regulations if only I could survive for another moment. Decades later when I read Mike Archer's account of the battle, *A Patch of Ground: Khe Sanh Remembered*, I appreciated that the attack had an opposite effect on some other men, who refused to believe that any god could allow such suffering to occur in the world. Nevertheless, as I listened to the earth-shattering cavalcade of incoming rounds, I felt terrified but also helpless to do anything about my fate.

Almost immediately, my eyes started to burn from tear gas, which forced me to rush back into the aid station and retrieve my gas mask. Once I placed it on my face, rather than gaining instant relief from the choking gas, I experienced repulsive claustrophobia and agonizing pain as the mask slowly cleaned the air inside. It seemed so eerie to be on a small plateau on the other side of the world from my home, crying, coughing, and retching from tear gas ignited by an invisible enemy dedicated to killing my comrades and me.

The shower of enemy shells raining down on us soon produced casualties who began to flow into the aid station. I rushed into the building to help the injured and found the pharmacy room on fire and on the floor a partially-exploded mortar round, which still had the Chinese markings on it. One of the chiefs grabbed a fire extinguisher and put out the blaze while we treated the casualties lying on the floor in the receiving area at the front of the building. One man's skin smoldered from white phosphorus (often referred to as Willy Peter), an awful substance that, untreated, burns through the victim's body, causing excruciating pain.

Suddenly, an ear-shattering explosion of noise, debris, and pyrotechnics devastated our base and introduced us to seventy-seven days of extraordinary physical and mental trauma as our adversaries scored a direct hit on the main ammo dump, igniting 1500 tons of ammunition—ncluding 11,000 rounds of high explosive artillery—less than 100 yards from our position. In the midst of the mass confusion of the dump explosion, one of the other corpsmen had been standing in front of the doorway. The blast picked him up and slammed him against the wall as if some giant had slapped him aside with the back of his hand. As I moved across the room to help him, I felt a funny sensation and looked up, just as the building collapsed. The force of the detonation and the falling plywood smashed me to the floor under a pile of lumber that had been our roof.

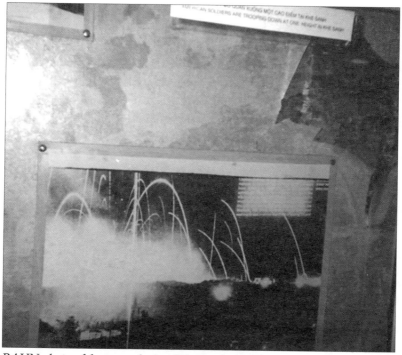

PAVN photo of dump explosion (Khe Sanh, 2005)

When I regained my senses, I awoke to a scene of utter chaos and bedlam as the doctor ran across the room pulling IVs out of the wounded men's arms so that we could drag them out of our no-longer-usable aid station and into the bunker. The man with the white phosphorus burns had a particularly difficult time as we used a canteen of water to moisten the gauze on his wounds so that the phosphorus would not reignite. Our small bunker swiftly devolved into a gruesome chamber of horrors filled with moaning, wounded men, and us, packed like sardines in the small space as enemy shells poured in and the tear gas returned. Yet this day's casualties would soon pale in comparison to the unspeakable bloodbath about to be thrust upon us.

When the shelling finally stopped, the absence of noise and the devastation wrought on our compound startled me. Complete buildings had disappeared while the rest of the area remained a total mess with damage everywhere. The live ammunition strewn around the base from the dump explosion presented an ongoing hazard. For weeks afterward, the rounds would explode or suddenly start smoking, leading us to scramble for cover. Even worse, an explosive removal team sent to Khe Sanh to dispose of the deadly debris soon found most of its members medevacked due to the constant incoming rounds, which exacerbated the enduring problem of our own ammunition detonating inside our wire.

Later that day, as we cleaned up the base and transported supplies to our new aid station, I suffered a light wound in another mortar attack. Our unseen enemy, knowing that we would be moving around after their initial attack, began randomly lobbing mortars at us, catching many of us in the open. I am embarrassed to admit that I received a Purple Heart for a very minor injury to my hand while other men paid a far dearer price for our commitment to hold Khe Sanh.

After spending most of the day establishing our new medical facility, we posted two-man watches in our doorway and retired for the night. I went to bed absolutely convinced that I would never see another day on Earth. We all expected a massive attack that night to overwhelm the base while we remained so low on ammunition. The next morning, I awoke utterly astonished that I had survived.

Regimental Aid Station (Khe Sanh, 1968)

My first day in combat and the worst day of my life had just ended— or so I thought. I had encountered the mass confusion of warfare and had begun to realize that I only knew the conflict taking place in my close proximity. The larger world and hostilities had little relevance as we braced for another, more deadly onslaught against our position. The war had become my personal battle, the one I still fight every night when I go to sleep.

I think this may have been the point at which my life began to go off the tracks. I asked myself what these guys had done to deserve this. The plight of the terrified and injured men who feared being wounded again, or buried alive in our tiny enclosed space, had overwhelmed me. I worried that my limited medical ability could cause them additional suffering and possibly death, while I remained more than mildly concerned that I could die as well.

As much as anything, my desire to learn why so many people wanted to kill us in 1968 led me into the study of the Vietnam War. But it also produced great skepticism in me about regulations and the people who make up the system. Indeed, rule-makers organized the system that sent us to Khe Sanh to fight a senseless battle in a war that they knew they had already lost. (While researching my doctoral dissertation, I discovered that the Johnson administration had carried out an extensive review of their Vietnam policies in 1966, and most officials had concluded that the U.S. could not prevail. Very few Americans had died in Vietnam by this point).

After witnessing the shattered lives and minds of men who had been wounded defending a country that later rejected them, I often asked myself, why should I follow anyone's orders? What would they do: cut my hair off and send me to Vietnam? They had already done that, and nothing could equal what the U.S. government and the Vietnamese did to my friends and me.

Ultimately, the war taught me always to challenge authority. Certainly, my contempt for rules and feelings of never really belonging anywhere after Vietnam sparked a powerful wanderlust. Almost instinctively I sense when I have been somewhere for too long and the time has arrived to move on. Hence, I have been constantly on the go since Vietnam.

In 2003, a professor and I organized a peace movement at Eastern Kentucky University (EKU) to try to halt America's headfirst plunge into a new Vietnam-style swamp in Iraq. In the midst of our organizational efforts, one staff member sent me an e-mail in which she accused me, accurately, of being a Liberal Democrat. She added, "There is no place in this country for people like you anymore." I have pushed the intestines back inside of a horribly wounded man, I have tried to ease the pain of men burned so badly that their skin peeled off like a pair of gloves, I have witnessed men become comatose from the constant deluge of shelling, I have collected body parts from the remains of two men who had run out of a doorway at the wrong time, I have listened to the screams of a wounded Marine as a doctor inserted a chest tube into his lungs without a general anesthetic, and I have abandoned wounded men so that I could treat those most likely to survive. And no place remains for me in America? I guess there really never was any spot for me after Khe Sanh.

PART I
KHE SANH

.

CHAPTER 1

Early Days

"Topmiller, I hope the f- - -g Viet Cong throw footballs at you."
- USMC sergeant

Now when I look back at Khe Sanh, I realize that I easily might have missed the whole thing, and I am not sure if that would make me happy or sad. I remain proud of my service but appalled at the damage we did to the Vietnamese and to ourselves. On the other hand, I have sometimes wished I had been killed in Vietnam so that I could have avoided all of the pain the war triggered in me and I in turn caused other people. I certainly do not celebrate Veterans Day and feel great bitterness when I reflect on the aftermath of the war. In fact, I am not sure if I can describe how betrayed I felt by the conspiracy of silence that followed the conflict and the negative images of veterans that emerged. Astoundingly, some American neo-conservatives (neo-cons) now argue that widespread stories about the ill treatment of vets simply constituted another liberal plot to distort history. But it did occur with stunning frequency, especially in the first decade after the war.

After leaving high school in 1966, I intended to join the Marines. While not particularly motivated by patriotism or a desire to serve, I remained convinced of the inevitability of military service and never considered the possibility of going to Canada or evading the draft. During the summer after my graduation, a group of my relatives came to my house to celebrate my exit from high school and my brother's impending entry as a draftee into the U.S. Army. When I told my collected aunts that I planned to join the Marines, they descended on my dad and demanded that he not allow me to go to Vietnam as a Marine. One aunt particularly related the story of her son—a U.S. Air Force pilot—who had taken a job as an aerial observer rather than bomb civilians in Vietnam. The next morning, my dad announced that he would not sign the papers for me to go into the Marines.

Thus, I joined the U.S. Navy in July 1966 at age seventeen under the Kiddy Cruiser Program, which allowed young men to join before age eighteen and get out of the military on the day before their twenty-first birthday. I felt a great sense of adventure, apprehension, and excitement as I left my home and my former life behind on the way to U.S. Navy Boot Camp at the Great Lakes Naval Station, north of Chicago. In boot camp, recruits had to specify potential career fields. My mother had been sick during much of my childhood, leading me to spend an inordinate amount of time in hospitals and doctors' offices. Thus, when I saw a listing for Hospital Corpsman (medic), I made that my first choice. Interestingly, the petty officer carrying out my interview had me sign the form to attest to the fact that I had actually volunteered to be a corpsman. Later, I discovered that the Marines utilized U.S. Navy medical personnel. But then it had become too late to reverse my decision and, anyway, I had "volunteered."

After boot camp, I spent sixteen weeks in training at the Hospital Corps School, Great Lakes Naval Hospital, across the street from the boot camp. In one of the ironies of the military (this war had more than its fair share) sailors who flunked out of Hospital Corps School often received immediate orders to Vietnam. Thus, it made sense to do well, because remaining in school at least delayed the inescapable orders to the battle zone. Following an even-shorter stint of field medical training with the Marines in North Carolina, the Navy sent me back to Great Lakes, where I mostly drank beer and got out of shape while I awaited my inevitable journey to the war. During that time, I gained some experience in bandaging minor wounds, mostly for sailors who got drunk on liberty and injured themselves.

My attitude towards the war went through a drastic metamorphosis during this period. The product of twelve years of Catholic education, I had left high school convinced that the U.S. had to confront Communism in Vietnam. But by the end of 1967, I had become an ardent opponent of the conflict. Nevertheless, I had grown up in a working-class family and had been inculcated with the idea that young men had to defend their country, even if many of my contemporaries considered people who went to Vietnam to be patsies.

Like many young people my age, in some ways I wanted to go to Vietnam out of curiosity and a desire to prove myself in combat despite my opposition to the war. Certainly, many of us responded to the idealism of the early 1960s only to experience the crushing cynicism of the late 1960s. Serving in Vietnam always made me feel that I was different from most Americans. Indeed, I agree with the late Vietnam War historian Douglas Pike, who worked in the U.S. Embassy in South Vietnam through much of the war and later argued, "There are only three kinds of people when it comes to Vietnam: Those who went, those who did not go, and everyone born afterward."

One of the most persistent Vietnam War myths claims that most Americans in Vietnam supported U.S. policy in the country. But it never really seemed that simple. Numerous people in the combat zone had severe reservations about the conflict but none-theless went to South Vietnam to fulfill their duty, or to avoid the wrath of the U.S. military, or the local draft board or the disap-proval of family or friends. Countries often wage wars on two fronts: at home and on the battlefield. Certainly, Vietnam became a bitter two-front war as many families found themselves torn asunder by the conflict. The domestic fracas that engulfed America over the hostilities taking place thousands of miles from its shores erupted in many homes, not just in the streets. But in the end, only a very small percentage of my generation actually saw heavy combat in Vietnam.

A few years ago, as I sat in a bar at the Navy Club on Yongsan U.S. Army Base in Seoul, Korea, one of my fellow faculty members turned to me and said, "The war really f---d up my life." Later on, he sent me an angry e-mail in which he wondered what had hap-pened to his universe when "The New Left had become the New Right." Indeed, during the 2004 presidential campaign, in the words of historian Chalmers Johnson, neo-conservative "war loving chicken hawks" attacked the patriotism of Vietnam veterans because some of us refused to accept the neo-cons' aggressive, adolescent, view of the world and combat.

For several years, neo-cons launched frequent insidious attacks against Vietnam veterans. In the 2000 campaign, the George W. Bush camp leaked rumors that Arizona Senator John McCain had mental problems as a result of his time as a POW in North Vietnam. After his election, Bush questioned the patriotism of U.S. Senator Max Cleland, who lost three limbs at Khe Sanh. In the 2004 campaign, the attacks against the Democratic nominee, John Kerry, escalated into some of the most shameful in American history as the Bush team tapped surrogates to question if Kerry had bled enough to earn one of his Purple Hearts and called into question events that surrounded his winning of a combat decoration. Astonishingly, delegates to the 2004 GOP convention wore pink band-aids to mock one of Kerry's Purple Hearts in a shocking—but effective—reminder of neo-con hostility towards Vietnam vets.

At one point, Kerry wondered aloud why members of the Republican Party who did not serve in the military had such disdain for Vietnam veterans. In other words, why did neo-cons love war but hate the warriors? I believe that their lack of military service led them to construct a fantasy world that they call the Vietnam War. Certainly, American neo-cons had so mythologized the conflict and its aftermath as to make it unrecognizable to someone who actually participated in it. In many ways, my current work grew out of my deep desire to counter this view by expressing the reality of combat and the long-term impact the fighting exerted on its participants.

Nothing infuriates me more than the neo-cons who now declare that they wish they had served in the armed forces. While I am continually amazed at how patriotic some people became when no longer eligible for the draft, I am astounded by the rank hypocrisy of people who did not serve explaining the reality of warfare to vets like me. Although the neo-cons have an infatuation with U.S. power, they fail to understand the cost of war because most have never been in the military and have no idea about the nature of military service. They remain mesmerized by American power to the exclusion of everything and everyone else, while their refusal to serve in Vietnam and their later willingness to send American soldiers around the world to support their combat fantasies symbolized the ultimate triumph of cynicism. Indeed, although many claimed that they supported the Vietnam War, most neither fought for their country nor joined the peace movement. Instead, they played it safe and sat out the fighting and then later evolved into super hawks when the draft no longer had the ability to place them in danger.

In the astonishing flight from reality that guides their rhetoric, some neo-cons argued that the antiwar movement led to the Cambodian holocaust, that the peace movement—not the war itself—caused many vets to suffer from Post Traumatic Stress Disorder (PTSD), and also that PSTD did not really exist. Instead, they maintained that PTSD represented a liberal plot to end a war that many of them went to incredible lengths to avoid. At the same time, they refused to acknowledge that the peace movement attempted to stop a conflict that many now agree constituted a terrible American blunder.

George W. Bush particularly displayed the neo-con approach to Vietnam. After using his family connections to join the National Guard and evade military service in Vietnam, he said decades later that he had wanted to go to Vietnam. The military seldom discouraged people from volunteering for combat duty. He could have gone on active duty if he really had wanted to go to the war zone, and I feel sure that a place would have been found for him to serve. Even worse, despite his deserter status during the war, he acted like a born-again John Wayne, landing on an aircraft carrier to confirm to the world his toughness and bravado. Astonishingly, when asked about troop levels in Iraq during the summer of 2003, the deserter-in-chief dared Iraqi insurgents to attack American forces with his infamous "bring them on" rejoinder. Who does he think belongs to this army? These are our children, not a bunch of mercenaries. His tough talk may make him feel robust, but it has cost many of our soldiers their lives. But, of course, he does not understand that because he never served in the active military. Ironically, I watched the press conference where he invited Iraqi insurgents to attack our forces from a hotel in Vietnam, where I had spent an excruciating summer investigating the continuing Agent Orange assault on the children of Vietnam.

Dick Cheney projected an even more extreme example of the war-loving chicken hawk. He sought multiple draft exemptions during the conflict because, in his words, "I had other priorities." So did the 58,000 Americans who died in Vietnam. Incredibly, neo-cons often responded to inquiries about their lack of military service yet willingness to send our young people to die fighting for a country they refused to defend by challenging the patriotism of the combat vets who raised the questions. Have we lost our souls as a people when we fail to be outraged when draft dodgers attack the patriotism of combat vets and get away with it?

Great Lakes—1967

The U.S. military in the 1960s bore little resemblance to the neo-con concept of the armed forces. In the months before I left for Vietnam, I began to notice some of the more troubling aspects of service life. One of my recurrent duties consisted of manning a dispensary at Great Lakes. Almost nightly, the Shore Patrol delivered men who had been arrested in Chicago, usually because of their Unauthorized Absence (UA) status, to our medical facility. Many of the prisoners had been badly beaten, while others demonstrated the obvious effects of hard drug use. I had never been exposed to opiates and other drugs, so I felt truly stunned when I witnessed the horrible symptoms of heroin withdrawal in our patients. The brutality of the Marine guards, who took custody of the prisoners once they came aboard our base, also shocked me. Often, they drove prisoners to their knees with the force of their clubs for the most minor infractions. Even at the tender age of eighteen, I marveled at the incongruity of giving someone a physical exam to make sure he remained sufficiently healthy to have the hell beat out of him.

But 1967 represented an angry year in America as opposition and disillusionment with the war grew alongside escalating racial tensions. Certainly, the U.S. military, which at that time reflected American society in general, suffered from the same pressures. Indeed, when I first arrived at Great Lakes, our commanders would not allow us to go on liberty without donning our uniforms. Two years afterward, they strongly discouraged us from wearing our uniforms off base because of the growing anger in the country over the war.

People preparing to go to Vietnam felt particularly resigned to their plight. At the same time, a sensation of disquiet and hostility seemed present among all of the returning combat veterans in our organization. A 3rd Class Corpsman in our dispensary who had been awarded a Bronze Star in Vietnam for escaping from a VC unit had been placed on restriction for drinking on duty soon after he returned to the U.S. He took advantage of his punishment to stand other people's watches in exchange for money. A career sailor, he feared that the malaria he had contracted in Vietnam would render him unable to complete his military career.

Many of the returning combat vets had drinking and discipline problems. They seemed to resent authority and projected an image of profound disaffection. My supervisor, a chief petty officer, had received a Bronze Star and a Purple Heart during the Korean War. We all respected him immensely because of his heroism, but he also displayed an almost utter disdain for authority and the military and had a wild temper, another trait that I noted in many of the combat veterans, and myself, after the war.

When I returned to Great Lakes Naval Hospital after my service in Vietnam, I lived in a barracks full of combat vets for close to a year. Just about everyone drank in excess and seemed astonishingly alienated and angry. Many would go on drunken binges during which they would become extremely violent and, in some cases, suicidal. The presence of hundreds of severely wounded Marines and sailors at the hospital did little to raise our spirits.

Okinawa/Danang

Great Lakes did not represent an especially attractive location, but the alternative seemed far worse. Nevertheless, the day finally arrived during the fall of 1967 when many of us received our orders to Vietnam. Several weeks later, after a thirty-day leave, a group of us landed on Okinawa, a small island south of Japan that the U.S. retained almost as a military colony from the end of WWII until the early 1970s. We thought that we would soon travel to Vietnam, but the people in charge pulled us off the plane to complete two months of intensive field training. Apparently, so many corpsmen had been killed in Vietnam that the USMC decided to toughen us up by exposing us to the tender mercies of a recent veteran of the carnage at Con Thien, South Vietnam.

We had experienced a brief period of combat training at Field Medical School in North Carolina months earlier, but this new instruction consisted of a far more rigorous and physically demanding regimen. Our sergeant, who stood about five foot four, tried to replicate Marine Boot Camp for us in the hope that we would increase our chances of surviving in Vietnam. Every morning before dawn, he turned on the lights in our squad bay at 4 AM and yelled "Good morning Navy" and then took us on a long pre-dawn run. We ran around a dirt track full of potholes, and numerous men suffered turned ankles and other minor injuries as they stumbled around the pathway. On other occasions, when our performance on an exercise had been especially inept, the sergeant would take us on a run along the beach, an intensely demanding undertaking in combat boots.

As time went on, we began to pride ourselves on the fact that we Navy Corpsmen turned out first for the daily morning run. In fact, at one point, after an exceptionally grueling jog to punish us for getting drunk and waking him up the night before, the sergeant had us stop in front of the chow hall as Marines waited in line for breakfast. Pausing for effect, he bellowed, "Men, standing before you are a bunch of pussies." Several of the Marines, especially the members of recon, responded somewhat vigorously to this assault on their manhood.

We believed that we had become so tough that we deserved our own flag. One evening, a couple of the corpsmen elected to play stretch with their newly issued bayonets. Unfortunately, one fellow missed and pinned his opponent's foot to the ground with his weapon. Someone grabbed a pillow case to wrap around the wounded man's foot after we pulled out the blade. That pillow case became our ensign, but we required a flag pole. When we suggested to the sergeant that we might go on a night raid to appropriate one from officer country, he responded, in typical USMC fashion, "Don't get caught." We did not and, thus, for the rest of our sojourn on Okinawa we proudly displayed our bloodstained flag whenever we ran or marched.

Although the training turned out to be totally irrelevant to my experience in Vietnam, I learned how to repel, made amphibious landings, crossed water obstacles on one-, two-, and three-strand bridges, and went to demolition school. The exercises carried differing levels of consequences if we failed. The one-strand bridge had a single rope strung several feet over water. We crawled on top of the rope, unhooked our rifles in order to be able to fire, and then had to hang from the rope by our hands. At that point, we had to swing our bodies so that we could catch the rope with our feet and then reassume the position on top of the bridge. While the exercise was strenuous and demanding, failure did not appear that serious; if you fell off, you just got wet.

The three-strand bridge hovered 150 feet in the air. As part of the exercise, our instructors told us how to steady a rocking bridge by squatting down on our haunches and stretching the ropes taut to stop the swaying movement of the strands. Sure enough, as we crossed it, our instructors started swinging the bridge wildly. The training worked and I steadied the bridge—but not my frazzled nerves—and completed the crossing. Unfortunately, one corpsman froze when the bridge began to shake and, not surprisingly, the instructors screamed at him and questioned his manhood while threatening to rock the bridge so hard that he would be thrown off. After an interminably long and tense period, he mustered the courage slowly to finish crossing. In a rare moment of compassion, the instructors refrained from shaking the bridge for the rest of his walk.

The slide for life had danger written all over it. Because so many soldiers in Vietnam had been injured jumping out of helicopters—at least that was the official story—the Marines created an assignment to show us the correct way to land in the water. The designers of the exercise had attached one metal cable to a large tree at the top of a mountain and another at the bottom. On the cable the Marines had attached a pulley-like device with two handles. The individual taking part in the training would grab the handles and launch himself off the side of the mountain. Part of the way down the hill stood a Marine who signaled the trainee when to let go of the pulley so that the novice would land in the water at the bottom of the hill in a sitting position.

Traveling at around thirty-five miles an hour through the air left little time to debate the wisdom or timing of the Marine when he gestured for me to release my hold on the pulley. But, of course, smashing into the tree that held the other end of the cable did not seem like an attractive alternative either. I came through it okay, but a few people had wrenched backs and other injuries from hitting the water at bad angles. When I returned to the island after Vietnam, I went on the drill as the official corpsman and had to pull several people out of the water who had sustained more serious injuries.

The first day at demolition school, an instructor walked in and handed one of our guys a quarter-pound charge with the fuse burning. Very casually, he said to the student, "Go throw this outside." To our utter astonishment, the charge blew up a few minutes after it had been tossed out of the building. Often, we asked our hard-charging sergeant if it would not be better if the VC killed us rather than him or his fellow Marines.

We organized a solid football team, made up mostly of corpsmen that participated in the base league. At one point, when we had a contest scheduled at the same time as a training exercise, I asked our doctor—the nominal leader of our unit—if I could be excused to play in an important game. When our sergeant found out, he called me out in front of the whole company and bellowed, "Topmiller, I hope the f---g Viet Cong throw footballs at you." On another occasion, when we complained to the doctor about having to run on Sunday, our theoretical day off, the sergeant made us march in close-order drill for hours the next Sunday.

We also attended Jungle Warfare School at the Northern Training Area. Our final task consisted of a night compass march during which most of us got hopelessly lost and a number of people suffered minor injuries as they slipped and fell in the jungle. Somebody came up with the bright idea that we should tie a rope around our collective waists to keep ourselves together. Shortly afterward, I heard some yelling and found myself abruptly thrown to the earth and being dragged along the ground after the lead man had stepped off a short cliff. I finally wrapped myself around a tree, which helped stop my headlong descent, but I decided never to do that again. Prior to the exercise, our leader courteously warned us that we might encounter the deadly Habu viper in the jungle and issued each one of us a sterile blade to incise the wound if bitten. However, the conventional wisdom held that the bite victim should light a cigarette if attacked because death would arrive before the end of the smoke.

Despite the rigorous training, at least, for the time being, we had avoided "going south"—a euphemism for Vietnam—although we still had to wait for a year to return to "The World"—the U.S. One corpsman feared going to Vietnam so much that he wet the bed every night in an effort to have the military declare him unfit for service in the war zone. I later heard that an armed escort put him on the flight to Vietnam.

On Christmas Eve 1967, shortly before many of us shipped out to Vietnam, a huge brawl with racial implications broke out in the Enlisted Men's Club. The degree of racial tension coursing through the U.S. military at the time rivaled civilian society in general, but I must agree with filmmaker Oliver Stone that we often fought each other as much as the enemy. However, we corpsmen seldom became caught up in the fighting; given that Marines usually would not mess with corpsmen since we often represented a wounded Marine's only salvation on the battlefield. When I returned to the U.S. in late 1968, the level of racial tension in the country and the military had escalated dramatically. At one point, many American bases in the U.S. had to be locked down because of the large number of racial incidents occurring throughout the military.

As we progressed through the training, many of us developed close friendships as only people could who faced an uncertain future together. Jimmy, an Irish kid from Chicago, became my close buddy after we served almost our whole tour together in Vietnam and then back in the U.S. His family took me in and treated me like family when we returned to Great Lakes after the war. Doug was another good friend and an amazing character. A champion boxer in the US, he once offered to rearrange the sergeant's face after we returned from a night of drinking in the village. We paid for that with a brutal run the next day. He won the Silver Star in Vietnam.

We all liked Howard, a kind and gentle Indiana farm boy whom I had known through most of my military career. He died in Vietnam from a gunshot wound to the chest. Shortly after I heard the devastating news about his death, I visited our medical facility in Dong Ha, South Vietnam. As I approached the hospital, I looked up and believed that I saw him walking out of the hospital towards me. In my joy, I rushed up to shake his hand only to discover that I had been mistaken. I wonder if I perceived his image because I could not come to terms with his death even after all of the killing at Khe Sanh. His loss just seemed way too close and personal. Another of our corpsmen, Louis, a Puerto Rican with a great sense of humor and a considerate disposition, drowned in Vietnam when his vehicle overturned into a river.

Adjacent to our mainly vacant base—most of the unit had rotated to Vietnam—stood a small village that operated mainly to service Marines and soldiers on liberty. I first encountered women of a friendly persuasion in the village and fell madly in love with one of the local prostitutes. She called me "Bobo," and we developed a deep affection for each other.

At least I believed it at the time.

Fortunately, maybe, I did not try to marry her, because that usually gained the budding fiancé a quick trip to the psychiatrist and an even faster ticket to Vietnam for those who persisted in their desire to marry a local. The obvious racial intolerance behind this stance did not go unnoticed but, in truth, many of us held deeply racist attitudes towards Asians, including Okinawans.

It must have been bewildering for Okinawans to see so many Americans passing through their island on the way to war. I wonder if they asked themselves why the U.S. seemed so willing to throw away its young people. After all, many Okinawans still expressed bitterness that Japan had pulled them into WWII, which had led to enormous civilian casualties when the U.S. invaded the island in 1945. Nor did our continued presence fill them with joy. Anti-American protests occurred regularly, which created great consternation on the part of military leaders who feared a sit-in demonstration or the seizure of one of our bases. On other occasions, groups of young Okinawans attacked or accosted individual Marines on liberty. And, of course, American military personnel assaulted, robbed, and raped innocent Okinawans.

But the greatest danger to us came from our fellow Americans. Next to our camp sat a small U.S. Army detachment that I long suspected had something to do with nuclear or chemical weapons. Almost nightly, serious fights broke out in the village between U.S. soldiers and Marines but also among individual Marines. The situation became so unruly that a squad of recon Marines patrolled the village at night to prevent more violence.

Years later, when I taught on U.S. military bases in South Korea, the behavior of some American soldiers towards Koreans never ceased to amaze me. Soldiers live in a world of violence that rewards aggression and assertive behavior. Is it any wonder that they cannot shut off their violent tendencies like a light switch? This seemed especially true in the case of South Korea and South Vietnam, where American soldiers, trained to kill North Vietnamese or North Koreans, then regularly mixed with South Vietnamese or South Korean civilians. Hence, much of the dehumanization and racism transmitted to soldiers to prepare them for combat ended up being applied to the neighboring indigenous populations. Certainly, a strong link existed between war, violence, and atrocity. Often when soldiers abused the locals, they acted out their intense training, just on the wrong people.

Going South

In 1967, of course, I had no conception of what lay ahead or of the atrocities that accompany warfare. Nevertheless, the time arrived to put our training into practice. In December, we began to receive our orders to South Vietnam. Most of the guys ended up going to the 3rd Marines, but Jimmy and I went to the 26th Marines. We did not realize it at the time, but our rotation to South Vietnam represented part of the American build-up at Khe Sanh in anticipation of the upcoming confrontation with the PAVN. Like many people who went to Vietnam, I left Okinawa and arrived in South Vietnam alone. When I returned to Okinawa months later, I had the same experience. I often thought that the solitary way in which troops were rotated in and out of South Vietnam contributed to our later alienation with the war and our country.

Of course, the harsh treatment of veterans during and after the war did nothing to lessen my growing estrangement from America. When I flew back to the U.S. at the end of my tour, the stewardess on the airline would not serve me a drink. In fact, throughout the long voyage home, the flight attendants studiously ignored the military personnel on board in a stunning preview of the coming decades in America. When I finally arrived in the US, as I walked through the St. Louis airport, a group of men still wearing their civilian clothes as they prepared to depart to boot camp, taunted me by saying, "Hey, look at the jarhead." I turned and replied, "Look at it this way. I just got back from Vietnam and *I am still alive.*" They did not respond. Even worse, during my first job interview as a civilian, the personnel director at a civilian hospital asked to check my arms for needle tracks. Given that I had been in Vietnam, she assumed that I had abused drugs. I had not.

Nevertheless, I first set foot in South Vietnam on January 12, 1968, after an interminably long and noisy ride on a C-130 cargo aircraft from Okinawa to Danang. Wartime Danang projected an otherworldly demeanor. The U.S. created an astounding Post Exchange (PX) economy in Danang with clubs, fast-food joints, grocery stores, and other amenities designed to remind American soldiers of home. Indeed, when I encountered a veritable mountain of beer that seemed to go on forever while driving through the city, I thought I had entered nirvana. Even more pleasing, American women—"round eyes" in our parlance—worked in some of the facilities, especially at the Red Cross canteen where soldiers procured snacks and other services. In addition, American leaders had thoughtfully created numerous drinking establishments to help us forget our participation in a war they had long known could not be won.

Many U.S. Air Force personnel lived, worked, and drank in air-conditioned facilities that remained off limits to Marines. Obviously, this bred great resentment as we observed the many conveniences of the PX economy not available to us. I realize that I may be alive today because of the courage of the air crews who flew supplies into Khe Sanh and attacked PAVN positions around our base but, even so, the Air Force standard of living appeared so irrationally out of whack in contrast to our relative poverty that it seemed hard to believe that we all belonged to the same military. It was outrageous to see non-combat personnel wearing jungle utilities and packing AK-47's in Danang when most Marine units remained dreadfully short of basic fighting equipment. Yet, the Marines prided themselves on doing more with less and the impossible with nothing. In fact, throughout the war, it remained a source of great satisfaction to Marines that they took much higher casualties proportionally than the U.S. Army.

Still reeling from the smell of diesel fuel and the heat and humidity of South Vietnam that assaulted my senses the instant I stepped off the plane, I flew to Khe Sanh the same day to report for duty. Although major fighting had not yet commenced at Khe Sanh, the last part of my flight proved harrowing given that crates of ammunition lined the floor of the aircraft, which made an unannounced and abrupt descent to the short Khe Sanh airstrip. In an effort to avoid potential anti-aircraft fire that might erupt from the ridges that overlooked the valley around the Khe Sanh plateau, Marine pilots generally glided along at a relatively high altitude, then dropped off the table, hitting the runway hard and screeching to a stop. Fortunately, the pilot had the good sense to ask us not to smoke on the flight, out of respect for the volatile nature of our cargo.

CHAPTER 2

The Regimental Aid Station 1968

"Here, you're gonna need this, Doc,"
- U.S. Marine 1968

I first discovered Khe Sanh when I deplaned from a C-130 on January 12, 1968. I did not even know the location of the impending calamity, better known as Khe Sanh, and could not have found it on a map. Everyone and everything had a crimson tint to their appearance thanks to the red clay soil upon which the base resided. After checking into the regimental headquarters, and being issued a rifle from a Marine who warned me, "Here, you're gonna need this, Doc," I walked down the road to the Regimental Aid Station (RAS).

When I met the doctor in charge, I found out that, due to my impeding promotion to Hospitalman Third Class (E-4), I had been elevated to the position of senior corpsman of the aid station, a standing that I remained singularly unqualified to hold. To think that my brief training had prepared me for what followed represented an absurd proposition worthy of a sadist and not the men who would come to depend on me. Little did I realize that this insignificant and isolated piece of earth on the other side of the planet would soon capture the attention of the world and reign over the rest of my life.

Our aid station consisted of four cinder-block walls sitting mostly underground with a plywood roof that jutted out above ground level. The facility had been divided into several small rooms and a larger treatment area. The first night, I had to sleep in the pharmacy that later went up in flames from an incoming mortar. I experienced such an all-consuming estrangement with my bizarre surroundings that I felt sorely tempted to take a Valium, which sat conveniently on the shelves of my sleeping room. But I decided against it because I feared becoming addicted to the medication. When I look back on it, I am amused by this moment of self-denial given that taking a sedative at that point would have been the least of my problems.

From the very beginning of my sojourn, I had to come to terms with the huge jungle rats that inhabited or, more accurately, ruled Khe Sanh. At night we could hear them running across the metal sheeting on the roof of the aid station. One wag named a particularly large rodent "big balls" because we could hear it dragging something across the top of our building. The first night at Khe Sanh, I stayed awake most of the night because I could not muster the courage to go outside and urinate and perhaps meet "big balls."

At the same time, everyone talked about the persistent problem of rat bites afflicting the base personnel. One of our corpsmen claimed that after suffering an attack on his foot one night, he arose, gave himself a rabies injection, and then, in a stunning display of coolness, returned to bed and went back to sleep. Yet, the rat bites also constituted a serious health and tactical issue. Some speculated that a number of Marines faked the wounds because getting the rabies vaccine, a two-week ordeal of abdominal injections, allowed them to escape from the field until all of the medication had been administered. When I first arrived, we injected the arms and buttocks of the victims who could tolerate the shots in their limbs, but after the number of patients increased dramatically, the doctor reverted to abdominal inoculations to discourage possible malingering.

Those first few days before the siege all seem to blend together now, but they return to me often in the form of flashbacks that created the mosaic that became my Vietnam in later years. We had open-air chow halls, an outside basketball court, showers, and many other amenities destined to disappear when the siege began. At some point, one of the units on the base put on a display of captured PAVN weapons and I posed for a picture holding a Rocket Propelled Grenade (RPG) to confirm my rather dubious tough-guy status for everyone back home. However, we all kept assuring each other that nothing ever happened at Khe Sanh, the safest base in South Vietnam. If I had known more about the brutal hill fights that our predecessors had waged to hold the area less than a year earlier, I would have had far less confidence in our relative safety. I made one brief foray off the base as part of a minesweeping team, during which I tried to stay as far away as possible from the radio operator and his antennas, which many of us referred to as enemy aiming stakes.

Shortly before the main battle exploded upon us, members of a recon patrol who had been badly shot up arrived at our aid station. Remarkably, I had known one of the casualties for a number of years in Cincinnati. He eventually filled me in with numerous stories about counting North Vietnamese trucks on the Ho Chi Minh Trail and life in the bush, including one account where he came across an enemy patrol and ended up opening fire after climbing up a tree trying to find his way. The latest action had been particularly hard on his recon team, which had sustained a number of casualties. The firefight also alerted us to the growing PAVN stranglehold on our position.

One day, while searching through a cabinet, I came across a performance report on one of the RAS chief petty officers. The statement noted that he had refused to leave his bunker to perform his duties at Con Thien. In essence, the writer called him a coward, a deadly appellation for a career military person. Yet, during the brief period I knew him, the chief exhibited great leadership and personal courage. He came upon me as I read the report and told me honestly that he had reached the point at Con Thien where he could no longer cut it and could not bring himself to leave his bunker.

I found his honesty disarming and shocking, but later when I had been in action, I came to understand his position well. Sometimes at Khe Sanh, I performed my duties and took risks that today seem extraordinary. Yet, on other days, I experienced a paralyzing trepidation that rendered me unable to move. I cannot really explain the difference but I believe that every human has a limit and many understand when they begin to approach it. This came home to me with dramatic clarity over the next few weeks as the constant shelling exacted a horrible psychological toll on many Marines.

In the days before the siege, we received increasingly desperate intelligence briefings warning us that as many as 40,000 enemy forces augmented with perhaps fifty tanks had surrounded us. Meanwhile, we tried to prepare for the dreaded and anticipated confrontation with the PAVN, but none of us had any conception of the catastrophe about to befall us.

One day, as I walked back to the aid station, I noticed a basketball hoop nailed to a pole on a space of open ground behind our facility. In keeping with my life-long love of basketball, I soon organized a game with my fellow corpsmen. Unfortunately, the base commander had recently ordered everyone to devote their free time to digging bunkers, filling sandbags and establishing fighting holes. After he witnessed our game and chewed out our doctor, I spent almost all of my "leisure" time filling sandbags to reinforce the small bunker we had constructed in front of the aid station. Despite the tedious drudgery of placing dirt in sandbags for hours, at least I was not in a rifle company on one of the hills that later became special hells for their defenders. I still find it mind-boggling that two of the three medical facilities on the base, which expected an attack momentarily, did not have roofs able to withstand incoming fire. Although some have argued that we did not have the sufficient lumber and materials to construct properly fortified bunkers, many of the Marines held the opinion that "Marines don't dig in" and thus resisted command efforts to increase their survivability. Within days, we discovered the great value of burrowing.

Seventy-Seven Days

As soon as we emerged from our bunker after the attack on January 21, 1968 (see introduction), we recognized that we desperately needed a new aid station. Before long the word came down that we had taken over one of the Air Force bunkers that sat behind our destroyed structure. The relocation to the Air Force position—what one Marine referred to as the Taj Mahal—turned out to be godsend for our wounded. Throughout the rest of the day, we moved supplies from the old aid station into our new facility. It was a superior structure featuring a long room, in which to treat casualties, that afforded real protection from enemy fire. A sandbagged roof and a stairway that had two turns reduced, the possibility of an outside blast killing someone inside. Unquestionably, I had a much more comfortable and safer Khe Sanh experience than almost everyone else thanks to the largess of the U.S. Air Force in protecting its personnel.

That morning a small man with an outrageous handlebar mustache walked into our new medical facility. When I asked,

"Hey, what do you need?" he responded that he was the regimental commander and wanted to look around. Properly chastened, I made myself scarce. Despite our rocky beginning, I must say that our commander at Khe Sanh, Colonel David Lownds, exercised outstanding leadership during the course of the battle. He constantly moved around the base, visiting troops and inquiring about our requirements. He insisted that all Marines wear flack jackets and helmets at all times and levied a fifty-dollar fine—a lot of money at our pay level—for every infraction.

When members of the American press visited Khe Sanh, they frequently vilified the colonel, sometimes referring to him as the "Lion of Khe Sanh," because they believed that he lacked the strategic depth to defend the outpost. Colonel Lownds did not help matters by acting like he really did not know what had happened at Dien Bien Phu. Incidentally, most of the press flew out of Khe Sanh every afternoon to ensure that they would not be on hand if the expected massive attack occurred that night.

The seriousness of our plight soon became apparent when we discovered that the dump explosion had reduced our ammunition levels to the point where each man only had his own personal supply on hand. Augmenting our despondency, within days Communist North Korea seized an American spy ship, the Pueblo, off the coast of North Korea, and the PAVN, utilizing tanks for the first time, overran the American Special Forces base at Lang Vei, only a few kilometers from our location.

I spoke to Colonel Lownds again in 1997 at a Khe Sanh reunion and I felt proud to have the chance to talk to such a great man and an outstanding leader (St. Louis, 1997).

Replica of Russian tank that overran the base at Lang Vei
(Lang Vei, 2002)

In both cases, our situation seemed even more desperate in the face of what appeared to be a worldwide Communist assault on an extremely overtaxed U.S. military. Many of us questioned whether we would be reinforced in the case of an enemy onslaught against the base given that U.S. reserves had slipped to a perilously low point. Adding to the sense of impending disaster, the Communists launched the Tet Offensive across South Vietnam on January 30-31, 1968. While Tet represented just another night at Khe Sanh, the radio dutifully reported that the American presence in South Vietnam seemed close to extinction. We waited in dismal expectation for a massive assault on our position.

Adding to the absolute horror of Khe Sanh, fog totally encased the base on many nights, reducing visibility to a few feet. Under the envelope of mist and darkness, enemy commandos steadily advanced their trenches towards us. in a classic replay of their successful tactics at Dien Bien Phu in 1954. The Vietnamese commander, Vo Nguyen Giap, who had been a history teacher before his military career and had utilized Roman siege techniques at Dien Bien Phu, now reintroduced the same plan fourteen years later at Khe Sanh. Even more shocking, a series of booby traps detonated inside our wire, leading many to conclude that sappers had infiltrated the base under the cover of fog. Eventually we supplied stethoscopes to Marines to assist them in detecting the tunnels that we assumed our foes had burrowed under our positions. Amazingly, months after we left Khe Sanh, we discovered that a member of our unit may have been setting the booby traps after his attempt on the life of one of our officers went awry.

During one of the early nights of the battle, we had to check the security of our bunker by venturing outside to see if any of our lights shone. As we walked around in the incredibly dense fog with our weapons drawn, I almost shot one of my fellow corpsmen who had literally walked up to me without my noticing. In my panic I had almost fired but, fortunately, he called out at the last second. As we walked back to our bunker, I felt a large rat run across my foot. After I kicked it away, the rodent came back at me and I got ready to shoot it. At the last second, my buddy reminded me that a gunshot inside the perimeter would have almost assuredly provoked a violent response from the nervous Marines on the base.

Often when the haze disappeared, all hell broke loose as Communist gunners unleashed a barrage of incoming fire on our exposed positions. One day, when the mist lifted suddenly, I heard intense firing and saw heavily armed Marines rushing through the base towards the lines to engage an enemy unit that had been spotted digging just yards from our defensive sites. As more and more Vietnamese dead littered our barbed wire, the base took on an indescribable smell of diesel and gore, and the rats grew fat and more aggressive from their opportunity to feed on corpses just outside of our lines.

The perimeter (Khe Sanh, 1968)

Eventually, we fortified the front door of the aid station with sandbags complete with firing ports so that we could lend a hand in turning back the expected enemy blitzkrieg. Many of us assumed that some part of the base could be overrun at some point and that we would have to fight the North Vietnamese inside our perimeter.

This seemed especially true for the Regimental Aid Station given that we sat on the narrow end of the base very close to the lines.

Many nights I, or one of the other corpsmen, sat at the bottom of the stairs holding an M-16 that I could barely operate, (and would have screwed up in case of an enemy attack), waiting for a PAVN infiltrator to throw a satchel charge down the stairs, from which there would be little escape. Rats swirled around my feet as I stood watch in the creepiest atmosphere on the planet. Often, I walked up to the top of the stairs and stared out into the fog straining to see any figure moving around. It felt so eerie and sinister that it almost defied description.

Unfortunately, our medical facility only had one exit, a situation everyone at Khe Sanh dreaded because of the likelihood that a blast in the doorway could trap people inside. As the siege wore on, several Marines found themselves buried alive when their trenches collapsed, but many survived because their comrades disregarded enemy fire in desperate attempts to dig them out before they suffocated. Our concern over being trapped underground increased when we heard that enemy forces dropped grenades and satchel charges down the air holes of the last remaining bunker at Lang Vei after they overran the base.

Everything outside the aid station represented violent, capricious, and sudden death. Yet, we ventured out on a regular basis,

Remnants of an American bunker at Lang Vei (1997). The valley below is Laos

especially to collect casualties or transport wounded men to Charlie Med where they would be evacuated from the base. Amazingly, people for the most part did not falter. Just about everyone attempted to carry out his duties; nobody talked about giving in or surrendering. While we had few options given that our adversaries had completely surrounded us and cut us off from the outside world, we retained a pretty solid faith in the invincibility of the U.S. Marine Corps. Often when conditions became particularly bad, our discipline and training took over and we muddled through.

And when we got a chance to hit back at our antagonists, it felt pretty good. The Marines believed fervently that "Payback is a mother f---er," which aptly described our collective mindset. After being on the receiving end of massive amounts of enemy fire, we thirsted for revenge and when we struck back—even with aircraft—we felt great satisfaction. Although military theorists and some instructors at the Navy War College raise nonsensical questions about ideas like proportional response and the proper amount of violence to apply to a given situation, the average Marine at Khe Sanh lusted for total payback. In fact, I would have nuked Hanoi if it had been in my power, especially after I learned about the fate of the "Lost Patrol" (See Chapter 4).

While we all expected a mammoth attack at any moment, by the end of the siege many Khe Sanh inhabitants ached to confront our adversaries in a cataclysmic showdown to end our physical and psychological encirclement. But, of course, that was what we wanted, so there was little possibility that the PAVN would grant our wish.

We did have several extensive conversations in the aid station about our duties as corpsmen if the North Vietnamese overran the base and captured us. The Geneva Convention required us as medical personnel to treat enemy wounded if imprisoned by the enemy. But the horrifying stories we had all heard about the fate of captured Marines at the hands of the enemy convinced me that I would run and take a bullet in the back rather than subject myself to the benevolence of the PAVN.

Nevertheless, the relentless incoming artillery, rocket, and mortar fire and the presence of enemy snipers who continuously shot at us made everyone nervous and jumpy. A simple case of diarrhea could prove fatal once any of us stepped outside to go to the latrine. Unfortunately, some tormented souls lost the ability to act, while my performance could hardly be characterized as functional. Simply put, some men collapsed under the remorseless psychological pressure produced by the endless stream of incoming fire, resulting in a high number of cases of shell shock. Moreover, everyone suffered mental trauma from the recurrent threat of being overrun. A Marine we had come to know quite well early in the siege because he often stopped by and told us funny stories about his close encounters with death showed up at our entrance one day escorted by another Marine. He had become comatose from the constant deluge of incoming shelling and had lost his ability to communicate in any form. Sadly, we evacuated him to Danang by medevac. I recalled from my training that psychological problems represented about 20 percent of all combat casualties but, of course, Khe Sanh was like no other battle during the Vietnam War.

According to the hyperactive base rumor mill, several senior enlisted men refused to leave their bunkers and perform their duties. One Marine later claimed that he walked into one dugout and threw a defused grenade at the feet of a sergeant just to see him run out of the foxhole. When another colorful character, whom we later dubbed Pig, declined to bathe, his mates gave him a bath against his will because they could no longer tolerate the stench. Pig emerged as a truly outrageous figure. Months later, when we occupied a hill outside of Danang, I witnessed him running through the compound one day waving a pistol at a rat fleeing for its life. Often when Pig drank too much, he passed out in his chair and promptly wet himself.

Incoming and Outgoing

Throughout the siege, a deafening pandemonium consumed the base as we incessantly received incoming and fired outgoing shells. In addition, huge U.S. Army 175 artillery pieces (the largest guns in the American inventory) frequently fired in support of our defensive positions from Camp Carroll, a base located about fifteen miles to the east of us. The enormous shells sounded like freight trains as they rumbled over our heads nightly, leading some of us to speculate on the very real possibility of a short round finishing us all off and sparing the PAVN the job of killing us. At the time, I did not know that the men firing the weapons had to put extra charges in their guns to maximize their range to reach Khe Sanh, which decreased their accuracy and increased the likelihood of a friendly fire incident.

Adding to the cacophony of noise at Khe Sanh, aircraft hovered constantly over the outpost as fighter jets, propeller aircraft, and B-52 bombers pounded enemy positions while helicopters shuttled supplies to the hills and our base. American airpower inundated the area around Khe Sanh with an incredible 103,500 tons of ordnance in three months, more than the total dropped on Japan in all of World War II. Additionally, U.S. aircraft attacked around the clock and, with their all-weather capability and advanced radar, assailed enemy positions despite terrible weather. Later in the siege, B-52's blasted Communist sites as close as eight hundred yards from our lines in a stunning demonstration of massive firepower: the trademark of the U.S. military in the twentieth century.

The arc lights (groups of B-52's operating in tandem) remained our most impressive and devastating response, although we never actually saw the aircraft. Each B-52 had the capacity to drop twenty-seven tons of bombs on a target. Alas, the deep rumblings of arc light raids—aptly labeled Operation Niagara by the American command—heralded massive destruction as a monsoon of death rained down upon our opponent's positions. One evening, our intelligence people discovered an underground enemy medical facility and pulverized it with an arc light. As corpsmen, we should have been appalled at the idea of destroying a hospital, but by this point, the idea of getting some revenge felt extremely satisfying.

That flying at Khe Sanh was extremely hazardous went without saying. When I first got to the base, the enemy shot down one of our fighter jets. The pilot successfully bailed out, but when our helicopter rescued him, the crewmembers saw North Vietnamese crawling through the brush trying to get to the aviator.

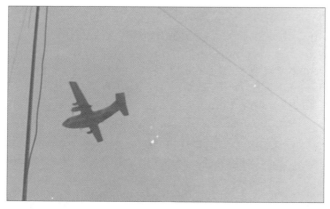

Aerial supply (Khe Sanh, 1968)

When the weather cleared, American fighter jets attacked enemy positions by diving towards the ground in a precipitous descent and then disappearing behind the hills. We saw the smoke from the exploding bombs rising in the air before we heard the noise. Suddenly, the aircraft screamed into the sky, trying to escape the fire pouring out of the heavy enemy anti-aircraft guns entrenched around Khe Sanh.

At times, American pilots attacked our adversaries with much slower propeller aircraft. One day, I watched as all kinds of debris, including foliage and bodies, flew into the air as planes worked over a tree line close to the base. Often in the morning, our pilots napalmed the trenches dug by our adversaries the evening before in blasts that produced massive displays of light, heat, and flames. Incredibly, some North Vietnamese soldiers rolled themselves into tight balls and covered themselves with their ponchos in a vain, but proactive, attempt to protect themselves from the searing heat of the napalm.

The bombing around Khe Sanh—and throughout the Vietnam War—demonstrated America's obsession with trying to win ground wars with airpower. Even though the U.S. had conducted exhaustive studies after WWII that proved the inability of bombing to break an adversary's will, American leaders still clung to the idea that they could force North Vietnam to sue for peace if they just exerted enough pressure on the Vietnamese from the air. Yet, we all learned at Khe Sanh that constant shelling and incoming did not break our wills. Instead, as it did in North Vietnam, it actually created a greater determination to confront the PAVN to settle accounts once and for all. We did not seek surrender. Everyone at Khe Sanh wanted payback.

On the other hand, we did not really know if we had killed anyone with our bombing and shelling because so much of it landed in heavy jungle. It seemed hard to believe that anyone could survive the astonishing firepower we directed at the PAVN, but they did, all the while demonstrating the incredible resilience for which the Vietnamese soldier became justifiably famous.

We utilized superior technology to meet the North Vietnamese threat as well. Electronic sensors dropped in the jungle around Khe Sanh targeted suspected enemy movements and triggered bombing missions. Advanced listening devices occasionally pinpointed suspected Communist headquarters, which also sparked our inevitable response. Khe Sanh also witnessed the extensive use of cluster bombs, which broke into small bomblets on impact and became deadly anti-personnel mines that continue to maim Vietnamese and Laotians. Meanwhile our snipers, at times using naval binoculars, scored numerous kills on unsuspecting enemy soldiers.

During hours of darkness, our aircraft and motors fired illumination rounds that highlighted parts of the perimeter in an eerie, fog-shrouded light as the flares floated slowly to the ground. Meanwhile, machine-gun fire punctuated the night as the PAVN probed our lines. Finally, in case a ground assault penetrated our lines, we had the dreaded beehive rounds that boasted the capability to fire thousands of small darts from artillery at a charging adversary.

We could also call on Spooky (sometimes called Puff the Magic Dragon), a C-130 aircraft that drenched exposed enemy troops with mind-boggling firepower from high-powered guns mounted in its doors. As journalist Michael Herr points out in *Dispatches*, the steady stream of tracers flying towards the ground from Spooky's guns possessed an almost hypnotic beauty despite the destruction they caused.

Yet, even this astonishingly lethal weapons system had limitations when utilized against well dug-in troops. One night later in my tour, I watched Spooky work over a rice paddy outside of Danang, flying back and forth distributing death to the poor Viet Cong irregulars crouching in fear below. Still, when Spooky completed its work and turned to leave, a long string of tracers suddenly erupted from the area where we all believed no one could have survived.

No system proved totally foolproof. Sometimes enemy soldiers crept up on our lines under the cover of darkness and turned our claymore mines around so that they fired at our troops—rather than at our adversaries—when Marines triggered them in response to noise or movement on the perimeter. Moreover, despite our massive bombing campaign, much of our firepower may have been ineffective because of lax security. Nguyen Chanh Thi, the former Vietnamese Commander of I Corps, claimed in 1997 that Communists had infiltrated the American and the South Vietnamese Commands all the way to the top, compromising many of our attack plans before the aircraft even got off the ground. Some commentators speculated that the Soviet Union may even have infiltrated our

B-52 bases while it maintained ships off the coast of Guam, where agents could watch American aircraft being launched and alert Hanoi to impending attacks.

The North Vietnamese held some advantages at Khe Sanh as well. Communist gunners attempted to shoot down our aircraft and shelled the airstrip whenever planes approached. They also deployed 50-caliber machine guns on the ridges above Khe Sanh, which enabled them to fire at our aircraft as they drew near to the base. Aiding their efforts immensely, our adversaries held Hill 1015, the highest point on the battlefield, which gave them the ability to observe our movements on the barren landscape below that became our base.

The Co Roc Mountains, across the border in Laos and beyond the range of our artillery, presented the most challenging target for our aircraft, because our foes had placed their artillery within its caves. Communist gunners regularly rolled their weapons out, fired at Khe Sanh, and then pulled their weapons back into caverns, rendering them almost impervious to U.S. counter strikes. On the day that our pilots knocked out three North Vietnamese guns at Co Roc, we rejoiced over our small victory.

Decades later, I ate lunch at a restaurant in Lao Bao on the Vietnamese/Laos border and actually observed the Co Roc Mountains from behind. I found it hard to reconcile the pastoral scenes of 2002 with the shocks of 1968. By 2002, the Vietnamese had begun constructing a modern highway at the base of the mountains and had established a free-trade zone just inside the border. Lao Bao reeked of wealth due to the extensive cross-border smuggling in the area.

At times when the Co Roc guns fired, we heard small thumping noises that alerted us to the fact that we had a few seconds to seek cover. Marines on the hills and spotters on the base fired red flares into the air as well to warn us of impending incoming fire. Although more deadly because of their greater range and killing zone, artillery did not seem as scary as rockets or, especially, mortars, which regularly landed on top of us before we reacted.

Discerning the differences between incoming and outgoing became the most important survival skill at Khe Sanh. Many of us developed what the American press labeled "the Khe Sanh shuffle," a crouching half-run/half-walk with one ear cocked to the sky to listen for the slightest sound of incoming while seeking out possible holes or trenches within which to take cover. Traveling above ground at Khe Sanh normally consisted of sprinting from one hole to another while carefully engaging in an elaborate psychological dance of denial to convince ourselves that there was no way another round could hit as close as the last one that had just barely missed.

Co Roc Mountains (Lao Bao, 2002)

One day as I returned to the aid station, three rockets landed in succession no more than fifty feet from me, yet I remained virtually untouched. On another occasion, I looked up and saw a six-foot-long rocket flying over my head. Once, when I heard the by-now-familiar sound of a very close incoming round, I dove to the ground trying to hug as much earth as humanly possible. It hit within feet of me but, miraculously, it did not completely detonate and I walked away again unhurt. When I bent over and picked up some of the shell fragments, they burned my hand.

One afternoon, we received an incredible 1307 rounds of enemy fire: one incoming shell every minute. Ironically, the heavy bombardment arrived so steadily in that instance that we took relatively light casualties because hardly anyone ventured outside and moved around. Nevertheless, the physical condition of the base deteriorated as the battle dragged on and more and more of the still standing, aboveground structures resembled Swiss cheese. One jeep received so many hits that the vehicle had over one hundred holes in it, so we dubbed it the "war wagon," after a popular John Wayne movie.

Despite our irreverent attitudes and constant wisecracking, the grim reality of daily life at Khe Sanh and the shellacking we had received on the first day of the battle created a constant sense of impending doom. Interestingly, many of us ended up hating the U.S. government and the U.S. Air Force far more than the PAVN for what we perceived to be their indifference to our fate.

One night early in the siege, Hanoi Hannah came on the radio and expressed her sympathies for the poor, suffering Marines at Khe Sanh. We laughed about it, but at the same time it seemed somewhat creepy to hear her conveying compassion and telling us that we were all doomed and going to die any day. Yet, the unforgiving certainty of incoming fire at Khe Sanh ensured that we could never escape the mind-numbing procession of wounded men who flowed through our aid station.

The war wagon (Khe Sanh, 1968).
PHOTO COURTESY OF MIKE ARCHER.

CHAPTER 3

Endless Casualties

"You should see the look on your face."
- Recon Marine

The impact of the fog and the ubiquitous presence of rats added to the almost surreal quality of the siege. It appeared that we had descended into some kind of primordial pre-human existence in which death remained the only option. Certainly, a great pall of depression and grim fatalism descended over us as we began to believe that it remained only a matter of time until we all perished. One doctor had referred to it as the potato masher theory: Eventually, the masher gets all of the potatoes in the bowl.

All the while our living conditions deteriorated as we waited for an attack that never came, and our overstrained medical services attempted to cope with mounting casualties. The medical preparation at Khe Sanh appeared inexcusable in retrospect, considering the U.S. command's preoccupation with Khe Sanh and the fact that a major battle seemed sure to occur there. The main medical evacuation unit and facility at Khe Sanh, Charlie Med, sat close to the airstrip, above ground, and had a canvas roof with sandbagged walls. Wounded men frequently braved intense enemy fire as Marines transported them to Charlie Med in an old military ambulance with a red cross on the side that served as a convenient target for enemy gunners. Men being medevacked out of the base had to stand by in a trench by the airstrip as they awaited evacuation. Once the aircraft arrived, they had to sprint onto a taxiing plane or be carried on by others. Many Marines received second and even third wounds; some even had to be returned to Charlie Med. Because of the fog, casualties sometimes had to be held overnight or for extended periods, thus denying them access to the excellent and far safer medical facilities at Danang and Dong Ha. On the other hand, we usually patched up less seriously wounded men and sent them back to the lines to aid in the defense of the base.

Moreover, within days of the battle's onset, we found ourselves bathed in buckets of blood as an interminable number of casualties flowed into our aid station. My uniform grew so caked with blood that it became as stiff as a starched shirt. Later on in the siege, when I met some new Marines arriving at the base, their shocked stares as they looked at my bloodstained trousers amused me. After all, I was a sailor.

Over the next few weeks, the gruesomeness of our tasks as medical personnel increased vividly as we ministered to hundreds of hurt men. I learned that caring for severely wounded men entailed far more complexity and psychological vigor than what I had learned about in Hospital Corp School or from John Wayne movies. Treating casualties sparked a mixture of revulsion, fear, and sympathy as horribly injured men with jagged body parts dangling by threads of skin screamed in pain while waiting for us to triage the worst victims first. Unbelievably, almost from the commencement of the siege, we experienced a severe shortage of whole blood and/or plasma and had to utilize blood volume expanders to prevent shock among our wounded. In addition, we had to prepare all seriously wounded men for medevac, which entailed inserting plastic tubes in their veins so that they could retain an IV while being transported. All of this activity occurred under barely sterile conditions, although we labored mightily to keep our instruments and other medical devices sanitary. Constant water shortages exacerbated the problem of maintaining acceptable treatment conditions for our wounded.

Members of the 3rd Reconnaissance Battalion (recon) arrived at our aid station regularly. Recon, in many ways, sustained the worst casualties in our sector because their bunkers sat next to the runway and, thus, they often endured heavy losses during the persistent shelling of the strip. I visited the recon area one day and marveled at their claustrophobic, spartan living conditions. As I prepared to leave, an enemy round impacted very close to the doorway. One of the Marines asked if I was okay and, in an attempt at false bravado, I assured him that I felt just fine. He responded, "You should see the look on your face."

On one particularly grisly night, a recon bunker suffered a direct hit in the doorway, trapping several Marines inside. Many of the ghastly wounded survivors panicked as they lay trapped in the bunker, covered with their fellow Marines' body parts, waiting to be dug out by their friends. By the time they reached our aid station, several had gone berserk. We stabilized one large, uncontrollable, screaming man only after one of the corpsmen injected a sedative through the Marine's trousers as four of us held him down.

One of the recon corpsmen had lost part of his foot. As we treated his wounds, I leaned over his body so that he would not see that much of his foot had been blown off. That night, for the first time, I experienced the putrid smell of the rotting human flesh of one of my comrades (The tissue around a shrapnel or bullet wound begins to die almost immediately, producing a foul odor). Indeed, the stench of gore has never completely left my consciousness. Years later, when I saw a photo of a Cambodian boy with part of his arm hanging off, I instantly recalled the smell.

On another exceptionally horrific night, we received a large number of casualties, including one Marine who had been wounded in the face. His jaw had collapsed, denying him the ability to breathe. The doctor performed a tracheotomy on him, and he survived only because one of our corpsmen, Jimmy, stayed up all night and aspirated the tracheotomy tube with a foot-operated pump. Sometime later, before the siege ended, the Marine wrote to us from his Naval Hospital, explaining that he remembered nothing after he had been hit and asking us to fill him in.

A badly burned corpsman arrived at our aid station in such intense pain that we injected morphine directly into his vein via an IV tube. He had been burned over 90 percent of his body and most of the outer layer of his skin hung limply on him. We stabilized him and all felt that he had a good chance for survival after we evacuated him. But when the doctor pointed out that his degraded immune system lacked the ability to withstand infection, which would almost assuredly result in kidney failure and death, our optimism quickly turned into depression. I believe that he died the next day at a Naval Hospital in the Philippines.

Once when we had wounded men jam-packed in the aid station, I worked feverishly to revive a badly hurt Marine only to hear one of the other corpsmen exclaim, "Hey, I think this guy is dead." We all backed off while he checked for a heartbeat and then walked away numbly when we realized that we had lost someone. In one of the more macabre aspects of Khe Sanh, we had no area to store dead bodies, so we placed the corpses outside until Graves Registration collected them. For Marines arriving at our facility, the sight of their dead comrades lying outside of the Regimental Aid Station represented a particularly gory introduction to the reality of Khe Sanh. Unfortunately, no one had the time or the resources to worry about the dead. Indeed, although the Marines are justly famous, and sometimes foolish, in their obsession to recover their dead from the battlefield, our trainers in Field Med School constantly cautioned us that "dead people are a supply problem." We ministered to the living.

One afternoon, as we sat in the aid station and listened to rounds screaming in, a Marine came to our door and told us that two Americans had been killed just across the street by an enemy shell. The sergeant relating the story told me, "They were just grab-assing, instead of staying in their hole. They decided to change positions and look what happened to them." I assumed that he conveyed his didactic history of their final moments to warn us of the dangers of moving around during incoming.

Across the street from the RAS (Khe Sanh, 1968)

The chief sent me outside to collect their remains in an empty sandbag, but I did not find enough body parts to even fill one container. When I returned to the aid station, I told the chief that I could not cut it anymore, whereupon he provided me a stiff drink out of his personal, and extraordinarily well-concealed, stash of whiskey. It did not help much, but I enjoyed the brief buzz from the only liquor I ever consumed at Khe Sanh. I thought I had reached the end of my tether, but so much lay ahead of us that I probably would have flipped out if I had really appreciated the horrors to come.

After a while, many of us lost all sense of time as we staggered through the blood and gore of Khe Sanh. Often I did not know the day of the week or the date; the constant shelling and the nonstop procession of wounded men represented the only consistent reality of my existence.

At one point, we had casualties throughout the aid station that had to be held overnight because heavy fog would not permit their evacuation. Suddenly, a short, grizzled, older man appeared at our doorway without the day's password. When challenged by our sentry, he yelled, "Don't shoot. I am the commander of the 3rd Marine Division." After the corpsman let him pass, he turned to me and said, "That's a good sentry you have out there." Then, in one of the more inspiring moments of my military career, he walked around our aid station and comforted each wounded Marine, inquiring about each man's welfare and asking if he needed anything. After he checked on the well-being of the Marines, he asked the medical personnel about our challenges and problems. When we told him that we had not received mail or pay in weeks, he became very upset. The next day we got our mail and our combat pay from the paymaster, who had been ordered to Khe Sanh by the general. The remuneration had no meaning for us at Khe Sanh, of course, because we had nothing to spend it on, but the married men claimed that they needed to obtain their salaries so their families could receive their allotments back in the U.S.

Food and Water

The constant demand for fresh water presented a great challenge for us throughout the battle. Although the Marine Air Wing and the U.S. Air Force devised a number of unique methods for delivering supplies to us by air, enough water to support the daily requirements of close to 6,000 men called for a local source because the volume needed far exceeded anyone's ability to deliver it by air. Our water point in 1968 sat at the bottom of a hill on the other side of the runway. Not surprisingly, the PAVN blew it up on a regular basis.

In 2002, I walked down the hill on which our landing field had sat. After hiking through rows and rows of coffee plants to our old water source, I discovered the small stream that had supplied us during the siege. It seemed inconceivable that such a puny little creek had kept so many men alive. Mike Archer later told me that the Marines had constructed a temporary dam in 1968 to collect more water from the stream. When I asked my guide why the North Vietnamese had not poisoned the water in 1968, he looked at me like I was a total idiot—that happens often when I am in Vietnam—and replied, "Well, they were using the same water." I considered asking him why did they not just get their water farther upstream but I decided to let it go. Hanoi plans eventually to dam the river and create a reservoir in the valley that sits below the Khe Sanh plateau.

Because water remained so tightly apportioned and we had to use most of ours to treat casualties, we experienced constant shortages through most of the siege. Towards the end of the battle, we finally received an exterior water container. One day, a Marine who had recently arrived off one of the hills asked me with absolute disbelief if he could truly have a drink of our water. In fact, the rumor mill claimed that some Marines on Hill 950 became so desperate for a way to brush their teeth that they applied aspirin to their gums, which, of course, had a catastrophic effect on their mouths and caused many of them to lose their teeth.

Water point (Khe Sanh, 2002)

During the battle I only attempted to bathe once, after the Seabees constructed a makeshift shower outside of our aid station. The shower, consisted of a 55-gallon drum heated by the sun, was operated by opening and closing a hose to distribute the water. Unfortunately, when I started to wash the accumulated blood, grime, and red clay off myself, the enemy showered us with a massive rocket barrage that sent me fleeing back to the aid station soaped up but not rinsed off. As I ran past a Marine in a fighting hole, he looked at me in my towel and flip-flops with a look of utter incredulity. The shower did not fare as well—we lost it in the barrage. Hence, we continued to stink to high heaven along with everything and everyone else on the base. When we finally abandoned Khe Sanh, a supply clerk in Quang Tri issued us new uniforms. Many of us stripped off the old ones on the spot and dumped them in a fire because they smelled so bad.

In the shower (Khe Sanh, 1968)

As a result of the lack of hygiene, I developed a disease that caused me to lose much of the pigmentation in my skin. The ailment seemed rather harmless, but I looked pretty goofy later on with my polka dot face. The condition disappeared when I went to Australia in June (their winter) and showered regularly with hot water for the first time in months. It came back when I returned to Vietnam, but then vanished after I went home at the end of my tour and sought medical treatment for the disorder.

Amazingly, many years later, I consulted a doctor because of a rash on my back that appeared after an extended trip to Vietnam and discovered that I had developed the same skin condition. I felt like something out of the "Twilight Zone' and, for reasons I do not completely understand, it sent me into a deep depression to be revisited by a skin disease in Vietnam after thirty-five years. The doctor declined to give me a fungicide because of possible toxicity to my liver, but when the condition came back again the next summer after another trip to Vietnam, I called a different doctor and told her how much the whole thing had freaked me out. Fortunately, she prescribed a fungicide for me that killed it—hopefully—forever.

Our missing beer ration seemed far more important than food and water in my mind. We were supposed to receive a two-can-a-day beer allowance but early on, the III MAF (Third Marine Amphibious Force, the overall command for all Marines in South Vietnam) commander declined to issue us our beer quota because of the risky tactical situation on the base. I have always wondered about this pronouncement. What did they think we were going to do: get drunk on our two beers and go over the hill? It was not like we could go anywhere and get in trouble. After all, the North Vietnamese had us surrounded. I suspect that the decision resulted from a lack of Air Force cargo space or willingness to risk aircraft to deliver 10,000 cans of beer a day. But the Seabees, the Green Berets, and the Air Force all had beer, which infuriated the rest of us.

Even worse, one day towards the end of our sojourn, two members of the U.S. Army 1st Air Cavalry Division (better known as the Cav) walked by our bunker eating steak sandwiches and drinking beer. Our sense of fairness received another jolt in knowing that the U.S. Army would not hesitate to ensure that its personnel had good food and beer but, somehow, the Marines always derived intense satisfaction in suffering more than the army.

More importantly, we also suffered from chronic food shortages given that the North Vietnamese destroyed our chow hall on the first day of the battle. Thus we ate c-rations (c-rats) for almost the entire siege. There were only twelve basic c-rat meals, and we usually only had two servings a day, so the variety in our diet remained extremely limited.

The culinary selections left much to be desired. No one could eat the disgusting ham and lima beans (generally called ham and mother f——ers by Marines), the scrambled eggs floated in a sea of grease, and even the coffee tasted weird. Fortunately, a new chief arrived at our aid station a few weeks into the battle who possessed an absolutely essential combat survival skill: he lacked a sense of smell and thus could not taste anything. Hence, only he could tolerate the ham and lima beans, so he offered to eat them whenever any of us asked, which relieved us of the task of gagging the meal down or starving. After awhile we became so desperate to vary our diets that we began to forage for food. To my great delight, I found an extra-large, unopened can of Chow Mein noodles in the remains of our chow hall, and from then on I ate Chow Mein noodles with every meal.

But at Khe Sanh, danger lurked everywhere, even in a mundane task like cooking c-rations. Marines were issued tablets that burned easily to heat our meals, but most guys preferred C-4 explosive because the stuff blazed white-hot and cooked the food extremely fast. One day, as I stood in the doorway of the aid station, I heard a loud "Whoosh!" I ran outside to see where the sound had originated and noticed a Marine lying spread-eagled on the ground about fifty feet away. I rushed over and saw that he had been scorched from head to toe. Already his skin hung limply on him, and he was in extreme pain.

The author in the former chow hall (Khe Sanh 1968)

We carried the injured man to the aid station and treated him, but I could not figure out what had burned him so badly. After we stabilized him, he said that he only remembered lighting the C-4. As I wrapped gauze around his mangled skin, I noticed a huge scar on his leg from a gunshot wound he had received during a previous tour of duty. Later, I walked back to the accident scene and realized that he had ignited fumes from an old gas tank that someone had discarded a few feet from his cooking spot.

Entrance and Exit Wounds

Yet, the procession of casualties never seemed to end. Over time, the daily violence of Khe Sanh dulled our sense of empathy or at least inured us to the enormous suffering of our injured. Perhaps that was the only way for us to endure the psychological impact of seeing our comrades arrive in our aid station in bits and pieces daily. When we trained to go to Vietnam our instructors emphasized the importance of rolling over injured men to check for exit wounds. But in the case of Khe Sanh we did not have many because shrapnel and concussion, rather than bullets, struck most of our casualties. But that created a whole series of other problems, because our wounded often had metal imbedded in their bodies, which meant we had to cut into their wounds, clean them out, suture and bandage them, and then endeavor to prevent infection.

In Vietnam the simplest wounds became grossly infected. Less serious casualties usually went back to duty, but often they returned to the aid station later on with gooey discharges and swelling around their original gashes that had to be incised and re-drained. This was a very painful process that further increased the danger of infection. Some men carried their infections home with them. When I rotated back to the U.S., I worked at Great Lakes Naval Hospital, which had a "dirty orthopedics" ward that held men with grossly contaminated wounds. An overpowering stench greeted guests the moment they stepped off the elevator onto the floor.

Wounds and infections only represented part of the medical challenge at Khe Sanh. Almost everybody became ill as soon as they arrived at the base, particularly if they had come recently from the U.S. Most developed diarrhea and vomiting because of the disease environment, the humidity, and the general bacterial level in Vietnam. We usually put them on intravenous fluids and medication to reduce their symptoms. And, of course, the lack of water contributed to dehydration, which increased the onset of diarrhea and susceptibility to other diseases.

At times, concussion from exploding ordnance caused seriously disfiguring wounds. One Marine standing close to the dump when it blew had the brains sucked right out of his head. His gray matter lay on the ground next to him afterwards. On another occasion, stretcher-bearers brought a man in who had been very close to an explosion that had ripped open his abdomen. When I saw his intestines lying outside of him, I tried to push his guts back inside, a very difficult task because of the revulsion involved, but also given their incredibly slipperiness. I realized that even touching them dramatically increased the danger of contamination and peritonitis. So I used gauze to shove his intestines back into him while another corpsman held his skin together. Then we closed the wound and evacuated him. As with most of the wounded I treated at Khe Sanh, I have no idea what happened to him afterwards.

One Marine arrived in the Regimental Aid Station (RAS) with a large hole in his shoulder blade. We always wanted to remove shrapnel to lessen the chance of infection but, in this case, I could not find any so I patched him up and sent him back to duty. About a week later he returned complaining about pain in his arm. When I examined him, I felt something hard in his arm and cut it open. The shrapnel had hit his shoulder blade and traveled downward, lodging in his upper arm.

Another Marine walked into the aid station with a bandage over the top of his wrist. He strolled up to me and pulled the battle dressing off, exposing a handless arm. The expression on his face pleaded, "My hand is gone. How do I get it back?" But I could do nothing. I put a tourniquet on his arm, bandaged the stump, administered morphine, and medevacked him.

A different Marine arrived in our facility with a sucking chest wound, the first one I treated in Vietnam. A sucking chest injury occurs when an individual has been wounded in the chest and one of the lungs begins to fill with blood. In the field, corpsmen covered the wound with plastic and a battle dressing to prevent air from escaping the lung and the rolled the patient on his wounded side to prevent the other lung from filling with blood. The doctor determined that the man could not be transported in his condition; he decided to insert a chest tube and drain the blood out his lung. Unfortunately, we did not have any general anesthetic and could not administer pain medications for chest wounds because they constrict veins and breathing passages and thus could prove fatal. Hence, we administered a local painkiller and the doctor cut a silver-dollar-sized hole in the Marine's torso underneath his arm and then started pressing the tube through the tissue into his lung. At that point, the injured man began screaming uncontrollably and, just as suddenly, his ambulance driver started shouting at the Marine to shut up and act like a man.

It seemed surreal: one Marine questioning the other Marine's manhood and reminding him to remember that he was a Marine, while the wounded man screamed hideously from the agony we inflicted on him. All the while the doctor forced the chest tube through the outer wall of his lungs, but the harder the doctor pushed, the more the wounded man bellowed. Finally the doctor hit the lung and blood surged out of his chest. Ironically, even though we had caused him unspeakable misery, we probably saved his life, given that he likely would not have survived a helicopter ride to a better-equipped medical facility. After we bandaged his wound, attached a bag to drain the lung, and stabilized him for transport, the same driver who had questioned his masculinity helped put the patient on the stretcher and carried him in the ambulance to Charlie Med to be medevacked.

Another Marine who visited our aid station had been wounded three times and got to go home. He received his third injury—a speck of shrapnel in his eye—as he deplaned on the Khe Sanh airstrip after returning from Danang, where he had been treated for his second injury. Although he spent no more than a few weeks at Khe Sanh, he still had to get on an aircraft to return to the world, which meant braving the murderous fire that descended on our runway every time a plane landed or took off.

His story was not all that unusual. Because of the unrelenting incoming fire, many men suffered multiple wounds, a fact that emerged as a contentious issue during the 2004 presidential campaign when some Americans questioned the validity of John Kerry's three Purple Hearts. Kerry's actions seem less sinister to a person who toiled in a medical capacity during the conflict. According to U.S. policy in South Vietnam, a serviceperson who received two combat wounds returned to the rear to spend the rest of his/her tour. Three Purple Hearts meant that the individual departed to the U.S. At the time, I understood that in general, the Marines awarded a Purple Heart for any wound caused by enemy action, but the U.S. Army required that the injured soldier leave the field to qualify for the medal.

But the real point is that just about everyone wanted out of Vietnam, especially after the U.S. announced its intention to open talks with the Communists in 1968. Why would Kerry refuse his third decoration and the ticket home that came with it? Some folks went to great lengths to get a second or third Purple Heart. One day at Khe Sanh, I walked up to the top of the stairs of our aid station and noticed that one of the corpsmen had his arm stuck outside the door. When I asked what he was doing, he replied that he already had one Purple Heart and needed to get hit in the arm so he could secure a second so that he could go to the rear and get the hell out of Khe Sanh. I responded by asking what he would do if the piece of shrapnel was as big as a rock and took his arm off. Swayed by my simple, survivalist logic, he quickly pulled his arm back inside.

When we treated injured men, we attached casualty cards to their clothing with information about their wounds, medication given, and other important details to assist the medical personnel who cared for them later on. Afterwards, I filled out a different form that I then sent to a Marine administrative unit on base that, I assumed, entered the information in the man's personnel file. Since casualties tended to come in handfuls because of the nature of the shelling, I hope that all wounded men received Purple Hearts, but I feel certain that we missed some people in the confusion and chaos of combat.

No doubt an officer approved the decoration at some point, but I am confident that officers routinely signed the forms considering everything else going on at the time. I obtained my Purple Heart because the doctor told the chief as he sewed up my hand to "Write him [me] up." It was that simple and absolutely no drama entered into the process.

But I did not get an award for the harm the dump explosion caused even though it damaged my hearing and caused me lifelong problems with ringing in my ears. However, I heard later that other people in the RAS acquired Purple Hearts for concussion while additional personnel received Bronze Stars for their coolness under fire, whatever that means. I know one individual who claimed that he earned two Bronze Stars in Vietnam, although, by his own admission, he never saw any combat. On the other hand, I saw enlisted Marines perform extraordinary feats of courage on a regular basis that went unrecognized. One Air Force reserve officer attained an award for bravery after he flew an aircraft to Saigon from the U.S., spent the night, and left the next day. He saw absolutely no enemy fire. I could never perceive any logic to the way the military awarded combat decorations, so I suppose that I should not be surprised about the controversy over John Kerry's medals. In recent years, two vets who sustained wounds at Khe Sanh but had not been awarded their combat decorations contacted me and asked for my help with their claims. One of the men later received his Purple Heart after a number of his fellow vets and I lobbied hard for him with the Pentagon.

Hence, I remain pretty sure that the under-reporting of casualties represented a much greater issue than over-reporting. And, of course, the military itself utilized numerous devices to minimize our true casualty levels, such as averaging the number killed to avoid public censure, or listing men who died outside of the base as not killed at Khe Sanh. In fact, just about every objective observer has panned the official USMC casualty figures for the battle: some 200 killed and 800 wounded. Even the travel book *Lonely Planet: Vietnam* scoffed at the formal count. I find myself becoming immediately suspicious when someone quotes the official USMC count. Often the perpetrators of this nonsense aim to prove that the bloodbath at Khe Sanh was overblown in press account as part of a larger effort to attack Vietnam veterans.

The Airstrip

While we had a tough job to perform in the aid station, others experienced far more harrowing duty in attempting to keep our airstrip open. Certainly, the runway became the focal point of the battle for Khe Sanh because it represented our only lifeline for supplies from Danang and other American bases along the South China Sea. Not surprisingly, everybody avoided the strip once the siege started, and when we heard aircraft approaching, we normally ran and jumped into a ditch because we knew that the runway would quickly be inundated with enemy firepower. Each time an aircraft attempted to land, the North Vietnamese opened up with rockets, mortars, and sometimes artillery; 50-caliber machine-gun fire also erupted from the ridges that looked down on Khe Sanh.

The PAVN efforts appeared successful at times. In the course of the battle the North Vietnamese destroyed several aircraft, including a C-130 transport that took numerous hits while still on the ground and then smashed into another vehicle and burst into flames. I treated one Marine who scorched his hands to a crisp, almost completely burning them off, as he tried to save the trapped passengers. He deserved the Medal of Honor, but I do not know that he ever got anything.

Soon afterwards, the Air Force decided not to risk any more C-130's and started sending in smaller C-123's, which could set down and lift off on slighter pieces of terrain. In fact, many of the aircraft did not stop when they hit the strip but only slowed down long enough to throw supplies off the plane and hustle replacement Marines out the door. Departing men and walking wounded had to scamper onto the plane, as stretcher-bearers darted onto the aircraft with their wounded charges.

Destroyed aircraft on the Khe Sanh airstrip   COURTESY OF MICHAEL ARCHER

The Khe Sanh airstrip (1968)

With the constant shelling, the runway became an area of great concern for everyone. In fact, the Seabees and Marine engineers constantly repaired the strip, often under intense enemy fire, and took heavy casualties in the process. The airstrip was unquestionably the most dangerous place on the base, or maybe even on the planet.

When it was all said and done, we lost a number of aircraft, including the C-130 smashed on the landing field, another C-130 shot out of the air with over forty Marines onboard, and three C-123's destroyed. The North Vietnamese destruction of our aircraft elevated our sense of isolation but also struck fear in the hearts of men who planned to leave the base soon.

One particularly heartbreaking crash occurred towards the end of the siege when the Frenchman who owned a local plantation decided to return to Khe Sanh. But, in an immense and tragic irony, as his C-123 taxied down the strip, North Vietnamese fire disabled the plane and he died in the subsequent crash. When the enemy continued targeting the aircraft, Colonel Lownds ordered the Marines to push it over the side of a cliff to avoid additional casualties from the incoming fire. According to rumor, this action infuriated the Air Force brass.

We also lost as many as eighteen helicopters. I treated the wounded off one of the early helicopters that crashed on our runway. They had only lifted a few feet off the ground when enemy fire slammed them back to the earth. The casualties arrived at our aid station in a state of extreme psychological shock, both from being shot down and from the force of hitting the ground so roughly. One story went around the base that claimed that a helicopter in the midst of supplying the hills lowered the tailgate for people to run off and actually crushed an enemy soldier crawling up the knoll to throw a satchel charge into the aircraft.

Frenchman's aircraft burning (Khe Sanh, 1968)

Airdrop (Khe Sanh, 1968)

Eventually, the Air Force balked at possibly squandering more aircraft on the landing field, so U.S. aircrews started discharging supplies by parachute. However, if the provisions missed the drop zone and we feared that the PAVN might capture the goods, our aircraft napalmed the supplies. Dropping mail by parachute supposedly violated American policy in South Vietnam because if the PAVN captured American correspondence, they allegedly wrote letters to the families of the addressees, an emotionally wrenching experience for people at home who received such correspondence. One day, after a mail delivery missed the drop zone, we heard that our forces napalmed the mailbags to deny them to the enemy.

A corpsman in our aid station once sent a letter home to his mother, who later informed him that the correspondence arrived with shrapnel holes in it along with a stamp that declared "damaged by combat." It made us all feel very battle-hardened. In some ways, being at Khe Sanh—the center of the universe—felt both exhilarating and terrifying at the same time.

If the airstrip did not seem dangerous enough, cargo flying down the runway rendered it even more hazardous. U.S. aircrews attempted a palette ejection system in which aircraft skidded along the ground and expelled the palettes out of the back of the aircraft with parachutes that deployed and slowed them down. At least one Marine died as a result of the palette removal system.

The logical move would have been to open up Highway Nine to supply us by road, but Westmoreland feared the heavy casualties that would result. Certainly, U.S. leaders never really designed an adequate supply system for Khe Sanh, a fact that has led many to question how, since the United States Military Command and Westmoreland wanted this battle, they could be so foolish not to realize how difficult the weather and enemy fire would make air supply. Khe Sanh sat on a plateau. When cool air descended from the mountains around the base and clashed with the hot air rising from the valley below, the plateau became, in the words of Ray Stubbe, "a fog machine," which further degraded efforts to supply us by air.

Although the runway presented an inviting target for PAVN fire, we believed that we also faced a threat from enemy aircraft. The North Vietnamese had never launched air attacks against American troops in South Vietnam, but because we sat so close to the DRV, persistent rumors arose that they planned to strike us from the air. Apparently, the PAVN moved some ancient Soviet bombers closer to the DMZ during this period, which made people in Washington fear an imminent air attack on our position. Obviously, the thought of Soviet-style migs strafing our airstrip and bombing the base, which remained entirely too exposed even for artillery, much less 500-pound bombs, left a tight sensation in many stomachs at Khe Sanh. On the other hand, it would have boosted the morale of our beleaguered adversaries, who had been subjected to our massive firepower for weeks.

Just when we thought our situation could not possibly get more unpleasant, it almost always got worse. At this point, I wanted to make sure that I clearly understood the new threat. I was in Viet f——g Nam which was bad enough, 40,000 bad guys had surrounded us, half the people on this base had been wounded, everyone felt sick, we reeked because we could not bathe, we had the plague, we did not have enough to eat, we remained desperately short of water, and we could be overrun at any time. I mean even Hanoi Hanna felt sorry for us. Now someone just told me that North Vietnamese migs might come screaming over that ridge and light up our airstrip?

They are going to bomb us?

It never ends here, does it?

Sure enough, word soon came down that the North Vietnamese had unleashed aircraft to strike Khe Sanh. As chills of fear ran down everyone's spine, the doctor decided we needed more security. He had us dig a dugout inside our bunker, no small feat given that we had to use sledgehammers to break through the cement floor of the bunker. Breathing cement dust in an enclosed space like our position was about the most disgusting activity on earth, so, in a funny kind of bravado and defiance, all of us corpsman declared that we would not enter the other dugout even in an air attack.

We heard later that when the PAVN aircraft approached the border, American jets scrambled off our carriers in the South China Sea and the North Vietnamese turned back. I have no idea if that story was true or not, but it exemplified the power of scuttlebutt in combat. When people found themselves in a traumatic situation like Khe Sanh, particularly when they had an experience like the dump explosion on the first day, they tended to accept as true just about any rumor. So we believed that an air attack would eventually strike our base.

On the other hand, our own fire presented a constant hazard. One day the Air Force decided to take out Luke the Gook, a PAVN soldier who sat in a spider hole at the end of our airstrip with a 50-caliber machine gun, constantly firing at our aircraft as they approached the runway. Hence, the Air Force launched a massive air attack right outside of our lines using bombs, rockets, and cannons to eliminate Luke. Afterwards, as one of the U.S. pilots performed a victorious barrel roll, we heard the sound of a 50-caliber machine gun firing at him—and we cheered for Luke! We thought it was okay that he had survived the attack, and by then we hated the Air Force so much we did not care. Meanwhile, several ARVN Rangers had climbed on top of their bunkers to watch the air attack. One of our pilots dropped a bomb on their lines, killing and wounding several South Vietnamese.

ARVN seemed to have inordinately bad luck. After we left Khe Sanh and relocated to Quang Tri, we received a briefing that we had moved out of enemy artillery range. The next day, as I sat in my aid station, I heard the unmistakable sound of incoming artillery. I lunged onto the floor, and a piece of shrapnel came through the ceiling and barely missed me. Vaulting out of the building, I ran outside looking for casualties. I ran up to one bunker and said, "Hey, are you guys okay?" A sergeant answered, "What the f—k are you doing? Get your ass back in that bunker. You don't belong out here running around." He must not have been at Khe Sanh.

We later discovered that a PAVN spotter had called an ARVN artillery unit with the coordinates of Quang Tri, one of our largest bases, and the South Vietnamese battery opened up on our position without confirming the directions. This added to my already low opinion of ARVN, a feeling many of us shared. But when I returned to Vietnam after the war, I discovered how terribly wrong we had been.

The Lost Patrol

At the end of the day, I always return to Khe Sanh and marvel at the continuing impact of that wretched place on so many Vietnamese and Americans. One day in February 1968—on what I thought for decades had to be the most horrible day of my life—a devastatingly wounded Marine appeared at the door of our aid station carrying another Marine over his shoulder. We had no indication that anything out of the ordinary had occurred until he walked through our door with his chin shot off. Shards of tissue hung from his face where his jaw had been, and a bullet had lacerated his tongue so that he could not speak. As I pressed gauze underneath his chin and started bandaging him up, he motioned that he wanted a pencil and a piece of paper. Someone gave him writing materials and he composed a note that—to our utter horror—explained that he had been on a patrol that had walked into an ambush and that a lot of Marines remained out in what we referred to as "Indian Country." We called the combat information center right away and told them that something terrible had happened.

That represented our first inkling of the disaster that had befallen our comrades as we all had to face the implications of Khe Sanh's infamous "ghost patrol." Indeed, anyone who served at Khe Sanh during the siege vividly recalls his location when the dump blew and when he found out about the lost patrol. Throughout most of the siege we seldom ventured into enemy territory because we feared being ensnared by the numerically superior forces that surrounded us. But for many higher-ranking officers, not patrolling seemed more dangerous than risking an ambush, because we never really appreciated for certain how many people waited out there to strike us. As Mike Archer pointed out in *A Patch of Ground*, although we knew that the enemy had "slowly surrounded" us, much critical intelligence could only be gained by a manned reconnaissance around our position.

In February, Colonel Lownds finally decided to send out a small detachment. To this day, lots of confusion remains over the fate of the detachment. At the time, we heard that the men traveled in the wrong direction when they left the base and walked into a murderous L-shaped North Vietnamese ambush that decimated the patrol. However, Ray Stubbe and John Prados argued in *Valley of Decision* that the disaster resulted from insufficient forces and the eagerness of a few of the Marines to grab a prisoner when they spotted some enemy soldiers. Needless to say, mass confusion occurred as the remnants of the patrol staggered back to our lines, followed by unadulterated outrage over the fact that many of our guys remained out there.

In the aid station, we felt extremely depressed over the disfiguring wounds of the Marine without a chin. Our dentist performed a nerve block that lessened his agony and assured us that the man's wounds would be taken care of with a prosthetic device and a skin graft. Obviously, we fervently hoped that he would be okay. For years, I stood in awe of that man who, for me, represented all of the young Marines who fought so selflessly at Khe Sanh and never thought twice about their personal safety as they sought to protect their buddies and, most of all, their corpsmen. I looked up to him as the kind of comrade anybody would want to have in that situation.

Decades later, I learned the harsh truth. After he returned to the United States, the VA could not fit a prosthetic device to his chin so doctors sewed his face to his shoulder and inserted eating and drinking tubes, an obviously debilitating condition. He later committed suicide, all because he had followed the most sacred USMC creed: Marines never left people behind. The day in 1997 when I learned about his demise also became one of the worst days of my life. I did not even know his name, yet I had marveled at his courage for years only to discover that he had really died in Vietnam, even though we did not know it at the time. I doubt that his name made it onto the wall, but it ought to be.

Discovering that so many Marines still lay out there constituted an even more ghastly aspect of the incident. We soon learned that the patrol had been slaughtered and that the surviving Marines had to make their way back to the lines by themselves; over twenty men had not returned. Later on, our aerial observers flew over the ambush site and reported the grim news that the North Vietnamese had lined the American bodies down the road to taunt us.

A great sense of indignation arose among everyone on the base that our guys had been left out there, but our growing desperation and depression heightened our sense of isolation and complemented our rage as we realized that we could not send out a platoon of Marines even a hundred yards from our lines without getting decimated. For many at Khe Sanh, that represented the lowest psychological moment of the siege, when we did not think our situation could possibly get any worse.

But, this was Khe Sanh, so it did. Soon, a major U.S. magazine displayed a picture of a badly wounded Marine from the lost patrol being carried back to the lines, which infuriated us even more because many of us wondered what the man's parents would think. Even in Vietnam an unwritten rule held that the press could not show American casualties, but in this case they did. Not surprisingly, because of the Vietnam experience, the post-Vietnam U.S. military became extraordinarily sensitive about pictures and information during wartime.

More importantly, geopolitics did not mean very much when our comrades remained in "Indian country." We wanted to get those bodies back in the worst way, so, one day towards the end of the siege, we launched an attack into the North Vietnamese lines. Many people thought that the siege had wound down quite a bit and the time had arrived to get our guys back. On that day, two of our corpsmen, Jimmy and Kenny, went down the lines and watched what they characterized as an utterly astounding U.S. assault.

Several Marines later claimed that when they sprang from our lines with fixed bayonets and approached the PAVN positions, they penetrated the North Vietnamese lines without being detected. One Marine told me he jumped down into the trench and saw a North Vietnamese soldier shaving; when the PAVN looked up, the Marine killed him. At first, the Marines gained great surprise and ran through the trenches shooting and killing people and satiating their lust for revenge.

Like so much of what happened at Khe Sanh, what started out as an innovative operation ended disastrously. The North Vietnamese got their act together and scored a direct hit with mortars on the Marine command post that had been established in a B-52 crater. The attack quickly dissolved and our people had to retreat. In the end, we took heavy casualties trying to recover the bodies from the lost patrol. I remember that day because it sounded like World War III, with bombs, artillery, mortars, and rifle fire all seemingly going off at once.

On a more depressing note, when the Marines started preparing to rescue the remains of the lost patrol, we discovered that all of the dental records on the base had been burned up in a fire. In one of the more poignant and macabre afternoons of my life, Marines filed into our aid station so the dentist and our dental techs could reconstruct their dental records. Although everyone recognized that the updated documents would insure that we could identify any of these men if they were killed, hardly anyone said a word.

One day towards the end of the battle in 1968, a Marine ran up to me in the aid station and told me that an incoming round had injured lots of men in the area where we discarded all of our spent shells. A group of Marines had been tossing our used artillery rounds out the back of their truck when North Vietnamese incoming scored a direct hit on the truck's cab, wounding and killing quite a few men.

After a screaming ride through the base, going through the curves on two wheels in the Marine's jeep, I arrived at the blast site to discover a total mess. The first man I encountered had both of his legs blown off and appeared to be in severe distress. Unfortunately, I looked about me and saw wounded men sprawled all around and realized that I had to abandon the seriously wounded man to go to the aid of the guys who had a better chance of surviving. The look on his face when he realized I intended to leave him has haunted me ever since. I have often seen his face in my dreams.

In later years when I experienced the bitter rejection by my fellow citizens, I often reflected on those desperate days at Khe Sanh when our comrades' bodies lay bloated, bloodied, and abandoned only yards beyond our reach. I wanted to scream and yell to break down the conspiracy of silence that followed the war but, alas, the taboo remained too powerful.

CHAPTER 4

Another Dien Bien Phu?

"Losses can be made good, damage can be repaired
and wounds heal in time. But the psychological scars
of the war will remain forever."
—Bao Ninh, *The Sorrow of War*

Almost from the onset of the battle, historians and commentators argued vigorously over Communist goals at Khe Sanh. Many of us who fought there asserted that the North Vietnamese legitimately wanted to take the base, while others maintained that the siege represented a massive diversion to distract American commanders from the upcoming Tet Offensive. These arguments may never be resolved, but the enemy encirclement of Khe Sanh certainly grabbed the attention of the American public, President Lyndon B. Johnson (LBJ), and the overall U.S. commander in Vietnam, General William Westmoreland.

Unbeknownst to most Americans, in January 1968, four elite PAVN divisions had already begun to surround the base while ostensibly preparing to overwhelm the position. Once the battle began, the attention of the world quickly focused on Khe Sanh and the possibility of a North Vietnamese victory over the greatly outnumbered U.S. defenders. Undoubtedly, the decisive battle of the second Vietnam War seemed to be unfolding.

Yet, the groundwork for the fighting had been established much earlier. Indeed, by the middle of 1967, despite his confident public assurances about American progress in South Vietnam, Westmoreland understood that the war would last forever if he could not force the Communists to stand and fight. He also realized that he had a limited amount of time to achieve victory before domestic opposition to the war and growing American casualties brought an end to the hostilities. He needed a decisive victory, and the French defeat at Dien Bien Phu in 1954 gave him inspiration. He decided to tempt the PAVN to engage in a conventional battle where American firepower could inflict massive casualties on the enemy and allow Westmoreland to claim a significant triumph over the Communists. In order to lure his adversaries into the trap, the base had to be weak enough to entice them but strong enough to repel an attack. Westmoreland wanted American airpower to make it a Dien Bien Phu in reverse.

Yet, memories of the French debacle at Dien Bien Phu had terrifying implications for many American leaders. In November 1953, after six years of stalemate in their struggle with the Viet Minh (the Independence League of Vietnam, a nationalist organization created by Ho Chi Minh to expel the French from Vietnam), French forces established a base at Dien Bien Phu, a remote outpost in northern Indochina close to the Lao border. Communist troops surrounded and eventually overran the base in May 1954, forcing France to abandon its quest to reestablish its colonial hegemony over the Vietnamese.

Ironically, French commanders had embarked on Dien Bien Phu because of their confidence that Western firepower could defeat the Communists in any conventional battle. However, the French greatly underestimated the Viet Minh's ability to mobilize its supporters. In an unprecedented logistical operation, thousands of Vietnamese civilians constructed roads through the jungle and transported artillery, anti-aircraft guns, and tons of supplies to Dien Bien Phu. The French remained so certain they could counter any Viet Minh attack that they placed their artillery in the open without redoubts or bunkers.

The French learned the unpleasant reality of Viet Minh capabilities on the opening day of the battle. Communist forces destroyed French artillery, planes on the runway, the ammunition dump, and several other positions with a devastating artillery barrage that continued until the end of the battle. At the same time, Viet Minh anti-aircraft units shot down numerous airplanes, including fighter-bombers, scout aircraft, and supply planes. French commanders soon found themselves outgunned, blind, and unable to receive effective supply.

When some observers pointed to the seemingly remarkable similarities between Khe Sanh in 1968 and Dien Bien Phu in 1954, the American press escalated the impending battle to spectacular theatre, with comparisons to Dien Bien Phu and extensive and sensational descriptions of the plight of the encircled defenders. For their part, American leaders hastily reviewed the Communist and French strategies at Dien Bien Phu while senior American political leaders recalled with dread and trepidation the humiliating French defeat that indirectly led to the U.S. commitment to an independent South Vietnam.

At first glance, the parallels between Khe Sanh and Dien Bien Phu appeared startling, but in the end the differences proved more important. Nevertheless, the terrain, weather, tactical disposition, remoteness, and desire for a decisive battle on the part of the Western force appeared almost identical. On the other hand, it seemed incomprehensible that Westmoreland had been sucked into the same dangerous situation that had doomed the French.

Increasing the intense speculation about the impending conflict, the Vietnamese utilized the same architect, Vo Nguyen Giap, to construct their combat plan for both confrontations. Giap personally supervised the Dien Bien Phu mêlée and, according to one of my Vietnamese guides, actually visited the Khe Sanh battlefield during the siege and narrowly missed being killed in a B-52 strike. Whether that actually occurred or not remains hard to say, but certainly he used Dien Bien Phu as a model for the destruction of Khe Sanh. Giap maintained a high level of flexibility and would have seized Khe Sanh if possible with an acceptable level of casualties. However, when we made a major move to hold the position through the utilization of unprecedented amounts of firepower against his forces, he shifted his tactics. In later years, Giap claimed that his forces prevailed at Khe Sanh given that the U.S. abandoned the base in mid-1968. Even more interesting, a Khe Sanh vet I encountered in Hue in 2003 declared that he had met Giap and that the general had insisted that Khe Sanh had not been a diversion to shift U.S. attention away from the Tet Offensive. I wonder why it is so important for Khe Sanh vets to believe that the battle was not a diversion. Does that make our losses more tolerable?

In the meantime, American perceptions of the struggle in Indochina had changed from viewing the war as a colonial struggle to seeing it as an important battleground in the immense worldwide competition between capitalism and communism. The conclusion of the Korean War in 1953 had allowed the USSR and the People's Republic of China (PRC) to rush huge amounts of Russian and Chinese war materials to the Viet Minh. At the same time the U.S. had taken a large measure of responsibility for financing the French war effort ($785 million in 1953), while encouraging and advising the French to hold the line against communism.

By late April 1954, a French defeat at Dien Bien Phu seemed assured due to the deteriorating strategic situation and the lack of sufficient airpower to supply the base. French leaders who recognized that they would suffer an imminent defeat without a significant increase in air power, viewed this impending setback with great alarm. A reverse in Indochina would give the Communists great negotiating strength at the upcoming Geneva Conference, deprive the French of some of their best troops, and possibly cause the defection of other French colonies, particularly Algeria. Indeed, the French position in Indochina, preserved at such great cost in blood and treasure, would be rendered untenable.

French leaders became convinced that only an American air strike could decisively turn the tide at Dien Bien Phu and appealed to the U.S. for assistance. Apparently some American leaders responded favorably to the request, although great debate remains over the sequence of events and who exactly offered what to whom, despite the danger of a devastating Chinese intervention.

At any event, American officials met with congressional leaders in April 1954 to request a resolution supporting a potential U.S. involvement in Indochina. The congressional delegation, which ironically included Lyndon Johnson, reacted with alarm. They believed that an armed intervention would contradict the lesson of Korea: not to fight another Asian action where U.S. troops did the bulk of the fighting. They expressed concern that the Chinese would intervene as they did in Korea in 1950, an action that could escalate into World War III. Insisting that the U.S. must not fight a war for colonialism, they refused to give the administration the kind of blank check that would be given a decade later with the Gulf of Tonkin Resolution in 1964. After much questioning and skepticism, the congressional leadership set three conditions for U.S. intervention: Any military action had to be in concert with U.S. allies, particularly the British so that the U.S. would not appear to be embarking on an operation with no allies; the French had to grant independence to the Vietnamese so that the U.S. would not be fighting to preserve the French colonial empire; and France must agree to continue fighting to placate the legitimate fears of the congressmen that the French would give up in Indochina once they had rescued Dien Bien Phu.

Meanwhile, a furious debate erupted in the American Pentagon. U.S. Army commanders demanded specific instructions and guidelines to match any possible intrusion and pointed out that American involvement in Indochina would eventually lead to the introduction of maintenance crews, supply, and security personnel to support air operations. They argued that an escalation of the fighting would involve U.S. troops in ground combat, would have to be accomplished at the expense of other U.S. commitments, would be contrary to U.S. plans to reduce from twenty to fourteen divisions, might necessitate an increased draft, and operations in the jungle would negate the U.S. technological advantage.

When the U.S. approached London, the British flatly refused a joint action in Indochina and made clear that they feared that an allied intervention might possibly lead to WWIII and that Indochina was not worth the risk. At the same time, after U.S. Vice-President Richard Nixon speculated publicly that the U.S. might be forced to intervene in Indochina, a firestorm of protest swept across the country, giving the administration a clear indication of the public mood and demonstrating that public opinion would be another obstacle to U.S. intervention.

Dien Bien Phu fell within days. The French government realized that its position in Indochina had become untenable and attended the Geneva Conference determined to withdraw from Indochina. Although the 10,000 soldiers captured by the Viet Minh represented a small percentage of the overall French force of 170,000 men, the psychological effect on the French appeared overwhelming.

The French concluded that they had been led down the primrose path by the United States and reacted bitterly. Decades of animosity between France and the U.S. resulted. President Dwight D. Eisenhower made a sound decision in avoiding a war in Indochina. Nevertheless, the U.S. commitment to South Vietnam grew to such proportions that later Washington planners ignored warnings that a U.S. military action in Indochina would be disastrous and unwinnable. Yet, by 1968, the USMC found itself facing its own Dien Bien Phu at a place the Marines never thought worth the fight.

The Real War in Vietnam

Indeed, the Marines had also followed a torturous course to Khe Sanh. Many Marines believed that the defense of Khe Sanh represented the logical conclusion of the flawed American strategy of search and destroy and another senseless bloodbath in a war known for meaningless sacrifice and destruction. In many ways, Khe Sanh symbolized the Vietnam War in microcosm. At Khe Sanh, Americans fought and died to defend an inconsequential piece of real estate, while the U.S. Command emphasized the military aspects of the struggle and ignored the absolutely critical political dimensions of a people's war.

The decision to defend Khe Sanh also grew out of a ferocious dispute that had raged since the introduction of American ground forces in 1965 between the U.S. Army and the U.S. Marines over the appropriate line of attack in Vietnam. Almost from the onset of American ground combat in South Vietnam, what I characterize as "The Real War in Vietnam" erupted between the Army-dominated Military Assistance Command, Vietnam (MACV) Headquarters in Saigon led by Westmoreland, who functioned as the overall U.S. commander in South Vietnam and exercised authority over all U.S. operations in the country, and the Third Marine Amphibious Force (III MAF) Headquarters in Danang, which directed all U.S. Marines and other American forces in I Corps (the northern provinces of South Vietnam).

Years before the debacle at Khe Sanh, intense debates had already arisen between MACV and III MAF over the correct tactics and strategy to implement in I Corps. Based on their long experience in conducting jungle warfare and combating insurgency in Latin America and Asia, Marines insisted that the war could only be won in the villages. Aware that they merely controlled the ground they stood on, Marine officers developed the Combined Action Platoon (CAP) program that called for small units of Marines and ARVN to live and work beside the villagers in the hope that they could forge bonds with them and deny the insurgents access to the local populace. Under the CAP program, in 1968 alone, Marine and Navy personnel provided 1,272,238 medical and dental treatments to the local populace, which for many constituted the first instance of modern medical or dental treatment in the their lifetime.

As the most experienced American counter-insurgency force, the Marines reacted with shock and consternation to

Westmoreland's decision to abandon the villages. The Leathernecks particularly objected to tying up their mobile attack forces in a static defense of isolated outposts like Khe Sanh. They saw the people of South Vietnam as the prize and understood that any strategy that lured Marines out of the villages would be counter to the American goal of winning the hearts and minds of the people.

Nevertheless, Westmoreland demanded that the Marines engage in search and destroy missions that sent large American units into the jungle seeking battle with PAVN and main-force insurgent units. This strategy exerted a never-ending drain on U.S. forces as they fought thousands of small, inconclusive actions producing numerous casualties and no measurable gains for the U.S. Marine commanders considered this a waste of manpower that bled the Marines by allowing insurgents to lure them into continuous small engagements far from the population centers.

Despite Westmoreland's subsequent assertions that search and destroy took the war to the enemy and lowered civilian casualties, it removed the Marines from the villages where they believed that the war would be won or lost. Marines later argued that captured PAVN documents alerted their commanders to a Communist plan to draw U.S. forces away from the inhabited districts to deprive them of the critical intelligence to be gained there. Marine commanders expressed outrage when they realized Westmoreland's strategy dovetailed with their adversary's plans.

Some Marines complained that Westmoreland's attrition strategy mainly wore down U.S. forces rather than the enemy, a situation the overextended Americans could barely endure. To compensate for the lack of manpower, U.S. commanders resorted to the one thing they had in abundance, firepower, resulting in more civilian casualties and greater opportunities for the insurgents to condemn the government of South Vietnam for introducing American forces into the country in the first place. Indeed, American combat operations continued in a constantly downward spiral, while Marines rightly condemned Westmoreland for a strategy sure to lead to defeat.

The feud between the Marines and Westmoreland, in many ways, betrayed the deep concerns felt by many U.S. officers regarding Westmoreland's flawed attrition strategy and poor leadership qualities, as well as the U.S. role in South Vietnam and the viability of South Vietnam. Some military leaders embraced the concept of an enclave strategy to lessen casualties and protect the vital urban centers and the U.S. logistic pipeline. Others criticized the use of body counts, the one-year tour, the refusal of civilian authorities to call up the reserves or mobilize the American public, and excessive civilian control of military operations. Many quietly worried about the prospects for an American victory in Vietnam.

Advocates of an enclave strategy appealed to American commanders to station American troops in the major cities, villages, and provincial capitals and quit rampaging through the jungle, taking excessive causalities, gaining zero, holding nothing, and protecting no one. The enclave strategy recognized the people as the prize and affirmed that political victory should be the U.S. goal in South Vietnam. Defeat for the PAVN, far from the population centers, had no meaning if it left the people unprotected and subjected to propaganda, fear, intimidation, and infiltration by Communist insurgents who used their nocturnal calls to gain intelligence, recruits, and supplies. While U.S. forces conducted operations in the jungle, in an exercise of extreme futility, Communists visited the villages recruiting new troops and demonstrating the inability of U.S. forces to protect them.

An unwieldy command structure added to the conflict between MACV and III MAF. Westmoreland did not report directly to the Joint Chiefs or to the Army Chief of Staff. Instead, he fell under the control of the Commander in Chief, Pacific (CINCPAC), a position held by a U.S. Navy admiral. As a result, Marine commanders, exploiting their traditional relationship with the Navy, often appealed MACV decisions to CINCPAC. Usually CINCPAC remained far more familiar with Marine doctrines and tactics and tended to favor them in conflicts with MACV. Army and Marine commanders also shared operational control with their ARVN counterparts, while no overall command structure supervised military affairs in South Vietnam. In the words of one high-ranking Marine officer, "the lines of command were hopelessly convoluted."

Finally, while conflicts between the U.S. Army and the U.S. Marines dated back to World War II, they reached new levels in Vietnam. Marines resented what they perceived to be the haughty West Point attitude of Army officers, particularly Westmoreland. They compared their own poverty to the seemingly endless supply train that supported the Army, while Army personnel bristled over the self-proclaimed Marine reputation for toughness and willing-ness to be "the first to fight."

One Marine later argued that Westmoreland projected an image of "the cardboard general, always correct in his actions, [and] studiously polite," while expressing constant dissatisfaction with Marine operations in South Vietnam. Westmoreland argued that Marine units were too heavy to carry out counterinsurgency in the countryside, measuring effectiveness by days spent in the field. Marine commanders, on the other hand, believed that Westmoreland remained so focused on the American experience in World War II that he exhibited a woeful lack of knowledge of small-unit operations and conditions in Asia. The Marines chafed under the ruinous strategy in South Vietnam, given that they still believed that the conflict would be won in the villages, not the cities.

By the end of 1968, relations between the two commands reached a new low as they fought over issues like the defense of Khe Sanh, the relief of Lang Vei, and MACV control of Marine air assets. These, however, seemed mild compared with the recrimina-tions that followed the American defeat in Vietnam and the efforts of both services to assign blame for the U.S. failure in South Viet-nam.

Westmoreland never grasped the importance of protecting the populace and thus lost the prize—the people—to the Communists. Westmoreland later defended his use of search and destroy and refused to accept the inappropriateness of his strategy. Westmoreland maintained that he wanted U.S. troops to take the war to the enemy while ARVN protected the people, a statement completely at odds with reality given that South Vietnamese forces gained considerable infamy for exploiting and terrorizing its citizens. He also felt that he could maximize American tactical mobility and lessen civilian casualties by fighting in remote areas. He maintained as well that he lacked sufficient manpower to protect the population and that with adequate forces, he would have adopted an enclave strategy.

In a weird kind of way, Westmoreland created his own enclave system. The extensive operations conducted by Americans in remote areas forced the U.S. to build a series of firebases to support troops in the field. These outposts became enclaves like Khe Sanh that could be cut off and besieged by the PAVN, resulting in under-protected cities like Hue and Saigon. Thus, insurgents exploited Westmoreland's shortcomings with the Tet Offensive in 1968, when they attacked just about every major urban area in South Vietnam and enjoyed early successes in Hue and Saigon.

Moreover, Westmoreland's strategy assumed that Vo Nguyen Giap was too limited in his thinking to deviate from his Dien Bien Phu strategy. Giap, who knew well the danger of settling into a fixed mode of operations, may have used his understanding of American psychology to mesmerize the American high command with the possibility of killing thousands of PAVN at Khe Sanh while he attacked South Vietnamese cities during the Tet Offensive. Even worse, Westmoreland lunged at the bait presented to him by Giap. Not only did he tie down good Marines at Khe Sanh, he held thousands of American soldiers in reserve to rescue Khe Sanh while Giap attempted to win the war for the people. Indeed, the best-trained, most mobile troops the U.S. possessed focused on Khe Sanh.

President Lyndon Baines Johnson (LBJ) may have also un-knowingly assisted Giap in his diversion at Khe Sanh. Concerned over the possible political fallout of an PAVN victory at Khe Sanh, LBJ demanded a written guarantee from the Joint Chiefs of Staff that Khe Sanh would hold, had a replica of Khe Sanh built in the White House situation room and demanded daily reports from Westmoreland on activity at Khe Sanh. Even in a war noted for civilian interference in military operations, this represented an unprecedented intrusion into operational matters and indicated LBJ's waning confidence in Westmoreland. LBJ's actions assured that the U.S. command would mainly focus on Khe Sanh.

Thus, the Marines defended a position and strategy at Khe Sanh that few believed in. Now when I look back on it, I am struck that someone chose to sacrifice us for such a worthless piece of ground. More importantly, I often wonder: Why did we let the U.S. government and military discard our lives? Yet, I understand now that our losses paled in comparison to those inflicted on the South Vietnamese during and especially after the war. I spent years attempting to make sense out of our terrible losses until I began to realize that I could only come to terms with Khe Sanh by returning there and confronting that awful place. My journey to peace and reconciliation commenced in 1996.

CHAPTER 5

Confronting Khe Sanh

"The American and South Vietnamese units are rushing to the
helicopters to run away from the Khe Sanh hell."
- Khe Sanh interpretive center—2002

Twenty-eight years after the mêlée at Khe Sanh, I stepped
off the bus, looked down and recognized a faintly familiar red
tint on my boots. Incredibly and inexplicably, I had returned to
Khe Sanh after almost three decades despite the fact that, for
many years, it had represented a terrifying enigma to me: a
grotesque hell full of death and destruction that took lives in a
random, horrifying manner. Yet here I stood once more on the
same red soil.

I could not say for sure in 1996, or now really, why I had such
a strong attraction to the hideousness I recalled as Khe Sanh.
Certainly I felt curiosity about the spot where so much killing and
devastation had occurred, but on a deeper, more visceral level, the
country had compellingly called me back to settle the unfinished
business of war. Somehow, I sensed a deep internal desire to finally
to confront the fighting where it had occurred so that I might shake
loose from the emotional straightjacket of the conflict.

It began innocently enough. In 1996, I flew to Vietnam to
conduct research on my doctoral dissertation. While I spent most of
my time in Ho Chi Minh City (the former Saigon), I scheduled two
days in Hue so that I might make a day trip to Khe Sanh. I had
assured my wife before leaving the U.S. that I would avoid Khe
Sanh to allay her fears that it would exact too great an emotional
toll on me. In some ways, I also assured myself that I would steer
clear of the experience, but somewhere lurking deep in my con-

sciousness, a voice told me that I could not pass on an opportunity to visit the old base.

First, I had to familiarize myself with Hue City, the location of a fierce battle between the PAVN and U.S. Marines in 1968. During the early years of the American War, Hue represented a special hotbed of Vietnamese nationalism that exemplified South Vietnamese anti-Americanism before 1968. Hue also had great strategic value because of its closeness to the Demilitarized Zone (DMZ) between North and South Vietnam. American and South Vietnamese (Army of the Republic of Vietnam, commonly referred to as ARVN) military leaders worried continually about a possible North Vietnamese invasion across the demarcation line to separate the area from the rest of the country. In later years, the region witnessed the most sustained and concentrated fighting of the conflict.

Ironically, Hue later evolved into the most pro-American and anti-Communist area in postwar Vietnam. During the Tet Offensive of 1968, PAVN forces seized and held the city for several weeks. After U.S. Marines recaptured the city in 1968, they discovered that the Communists had executed several thousand innocent civilians. Unbearably, by the time of my return, the people of Hue had lived for over a quarter-century under the authority of a party that they know slaughtered their friends, relatives, and neighbors. Indeed, the police and military presence in the city remained overwhelming even in the twenty-first century in a clear attempt to intimidate the regime's potential opponents. At one point, when I suggested to one of my guides that she simply ask the police the address of an individual I wanted to interview, the terror on her face amply demonstrated the pervasive fear of the Communists that many Vietnamese still experience.

Historian Douglas Pike once asserted that it remained impossible to ascertain the true nature of Vietnamese attitudes towards outsiders due to the clandestine nature of the Vietnamese people. By this he meant that the Vietnamese, through their long history of foreign invasion and occupation, developed a habit of self-survival in never telling foreigners what they really thought. Yet, I found Hue people particularly outspoken in their opposition to Communism despite the heavy penalties that could be visited on them by the Vietnamese Communist Party (VCP). Notwithstanding the fact that Hue became an important tourist Mecca in modern Vietnam, many of its citizens seethed under the domination of the VCP. As one restaurant owner whispered to me under his breath one evening, "People [tourists] don't know the real situation here."

Over time, Hue became my favorite Vietnamese city. Many evenings over the last decade, I sat by the Perfume River drinking 60-cent-a-bottle beer as the sun set and I marveled at the beauty and timeless serenity of Hue, the most lovely of all Vietnamese cities. The differences between Hue and Ho Chi Minh City seemed almost indescribable. Indeed, if Ho Chi Minh City stood for cosmopolitanism, youth, and chaos, Hue symbolized tradition, tranquility, and the eternal essence of rural Vietnam.

To Khe Sanh

When I arrived in Hue in 1996, I asked my hotel clerk about the DMZ tour, and she told me to be in the lobby the next morning at six o'clock. I spent the rest of the day touring pagodas in the Hue area as my excitement and apprehension intensified. While I still maintained a degree of sober lucidity, I met an Italian woman who inquired about my background. When I told her that I had returned to Vietnam by myself and would soon visit Khe Sanh, she exclaimed: "What a strong man you are."

Not really.

That night, I slammed beer with gusto, ending the night in a drunken stupor.

Finally, morning arrived. I arose at four and hurried down to the lobby by five, waking the desk clerk. After I had sat in the reception area for close to fifty minutes, he asked me casually if I had a ticket for the tour. When I said no, that I planned to purchase it from the driver of the bus, he ran outside and quickly hailed a cyclo. I took a very fast and nerve-racking ride across the city as I realized that I might literally miss the bus.

As soon as I arrived at the DMZ tour office, the manager barked out orders to two young men who hurriedly jumped on motorcycles and sped away from the office. Only then did I realize that they had been sent after the bus. Following an agonizing fifteen minutes, the bus returned to the office, and I filled the last seat. The irony of my position struck me hard. I had traveled thousands of miles and waited twenty-eight years only to come within a whisker of not making it to Khe Sanh.

On the way north to Dong Ha, many of the pastoral scenes that I remembered about South Vietnam appeared: old women carried improbably heavy loads on their shoulders while small children sat astride huge water buffalo as the expanding countryside filled with rice paddies. I also began to grasp that the Vietnam I once knew no longer existed. I first encountered this sensation when I flew into my last duty station, Phu Bai airport, outside of Hue. During the war, we maintained a large base there that surrounded the present-day airstrip, but I never made it into the city in 1968 because Hue remained off-limits to Marines.

I had always associated Phu Bai with the huge U.S. base that had sat there at the time. Instead, no sign of the American presence lingered, apart from a few deserted guard towers and abandoned bunkers off in the distance. The Vietnamese Army had established a garrison there but, like many PAVN bases, it stayed hidden from view except for a sign at the front gate. As we drove north along Highway One, I encountered the same state of affairs. In my mind I had forever linked Dong Ha and Quang Tri with the U.S. airfields and hospitals there. Yet, they also had vanished. It seemed as if the Communists had determined that eradicating the last vestiges of our presence would allow them to claim complete victory over us.

Indeed, the landscape where so much fighting had occurred, to my great shock and dismay, appeared to have completely recovered from the war. Several years later, when I ascertained the human devastation brought on by Agent Orange, I realized that my initial observations had been mistaken. But at that point, it appeared as if the war had never happened and our involvement had constituted more an illusion than reality. At the time, it seemed that Vietnam, in its interminable history, had again recovered from another foreign invasion. Perhaps I was foolhardy to expect to return to a Vietnam as I remembered it, but I found myself unprepared for such a drastic change.

As I traveled northward, I noticed many large military graveyards, always adorned with significant monuments commemorating the sacrifices of the PAVN and Viet Cong (VC) soldiers who fought and died there. Across the old DMZ, a huge cemetery held the graves of over 10,000 soldiers killed along the Ho Chi Minh Trail. In my later trips, I would notice that the VCP increasingly located its local headquarters next to military graveyards in an effort to use the conflict to gain increased legitimacy for the party.

The war memorials called forth one of the more extreme ironies of the Vietnam War. The VCP had struggled for years with

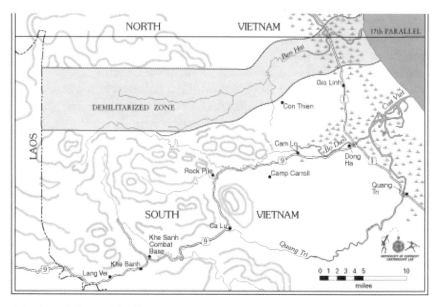

Northern I Corps (1968)
COURTESY OF DICK GILBREATH, U. K.

the realization that despite the party's repeated and tedious efforts to remind the people that it defeated the Americans and the French, over 50 percent of the population of Vietnam was born after 1975 and cared little about the hostilities. Indeed, many young Vietnamese mimicked American values and cultural norms while cash payments from Vietnamese Americans to their relatives in Vietnam and investment capital from Vietnamese Americans—who loathed the VCP—represented a major source of external revenue for Vietnam. Hence, Hanoi tolerated the Communist-hating Viet Kieu (overseas Vietnamese) to bring in enough foreign capital to ensure continued economic growth and allow the VCP to retain power.

Finally, we arrived in Dong Ha, the location of a large naval medical facility in 1968, where we picked up our guide, Hoang. Then we drove straight up Highway One to the Ben Hai River, the old border between North and South Vietnam. As we traveled northward I noticed far fewer people and towns. It seemed as if the people had decided to leave the area forever sparsely populated. At the Ben Hai River, I had the rare opportunity to view the old South Vietnam from the north bank, a sight I certainly never thought I would see. Before the conflict, both sides had maintained their halves of the bridge and even painted them different colors. We bombed the structure during the fighting, of course, but it had since been rebuilt. On the northern shore stood a huge monument commemorating the years Vietnam remained divided while declaring that, in the words of Ho Chi Minh, "Vietnam will always be united even after the mountains have withered away and the rivers run dry."

From there we drove to the coast and visited a tunnel area across from Con Co Island. Apparently, the U.S. leveled the city that sat there at the beginning of the war, so the North Vietnamese moved the entire population underground. The passageways covered 2.8 kilometers, and the base operated continuously during the fighting despite intensive American bombing. In fact, hundreds of bomb craters dotted the landscape around the complex.

On the way back to Dong Ha, as we drove through the sleepy town of Gio Linh, just inside the old border of South Vietnam, I could not imagine that seven years later I would visit a medical facility there that cared for over 129 children suffering from the long-term effects of Agent Orange in a chilling demonstration of the continuing impact of the hostilities.

Shortly afterward, we finally started up Highway Nine to Khe Sanh. I had never been on Highway Nine before, given that I had arrived at Khe Sanh nine days before the siege started and the PAVN held the road at that time. We first paused close to the Rockpile, an important Marine outpost perched atop razor-sharp peaks during the war that witnessed heavy fighting in the 1960s.

Six years later, when I stopped at the Rockpile again with another guide and a completely different perspective on Vietnam and the war, my guide commented on the high level of deaths in Vietnam from Unexploded Ordnance (UXO) since 1975. He told me that he had been standing on our spot once when he heard a loud detonation that had killed two local boys. As he spoke, a deafening explosion reverberated across the valley, which just about sent me into cardiac arrest. Fortunately, the noise came from a quarry where workers blasted rock that they used to repair the highway.

The danger from UXO remained very real in Indochina even into the twenty-first century. Indeed, the Vietnamese suffered an additional 100,000 killed and wounded after the war's termination from undetonated explosives. I encountered a similar situation in Laos in January 2004. American UXO—particularly cluster bombs—

dropped on the Ho Chi Minh Trail during the war continued to injure numerous Lao and Highland people.

Khe Sanh—1996

As we drove up the highway, the stunningly beautiful panorama of the valley that falls away from the Khe Sanh plateau suddenly leapt into view. My heart began to beat rapidly, and I grew increasingly uneasy as we approached the old base. Abruptly, the bus stopped, and I could see Hill 1015 out of the window.

I hurriedly walked up a trail to a bare spot of earth where I

Khe Sanh valley, 1997

stood on what I mistakenly assumed was the old airstrip. Our guide, Hoang, claimed that nothing would grow on this narrow piece of land, a statement that did not surprise me considering the amount of deadly explosives that I believed still lurked underneath its harmless-looking surface.

A local man offered to sell me various American insignias he had dug from the ground. The idea repelled me, just as in Ho Chi Minh City when I had observed displays of American dog tags in souvenir stores. Who would purchase these remnants of men who fought and died, I asked myself? But after I returned to the US, another veteran pointed out that some of these mementoes have proved valuable in resolving the fate of American MIAs. Now, I deeply regret that I did not buy as many as I could.

The Red Scar (Khe Sanh, 1996)

As I stood at Khe Sanh and stared at Hill 1015, feelings of sadness and regret overwhelmed me as I tried to remember all of the young Vietnamese and American men who died over what eventually became a privately owned farm. I felt robbed and cheated; surely there should be a memorial, some kind of reminder of the bloodletting that occurred here. When I returned to Khe Sanh the following year, I stumbled upon a large monument to the PAVN 2nd Division at the junction of Highway Nine and the road to the base but, of course, no memorial to the U.S. Marines, Montagnards, and South Vietnamese who perished there will ever appear in Communist Vietnam.

At the same time, to my absolute astonishment, I realized that the land had also reclaimed Khe Sanh. The base had been converted into a huge coffee plantation with the exception of an airstrip, which existed as a long, red scar on the land. The pockmarked hillsides, which had resembled the surface of the moon some three decades earlier, had also regained their lushness, a condition that hit me with stunning force as I recognized, for the third time in one day, that the Vietnam I remembered, the place that had resided so firmly in my consciousness and had ruled so much of my life, simply no longer existed. The land and the people had told me to move on, to adapt or perish. But I found myself unable to make such a dramatic leap in my confused and frenzied state. At one point, I muttered to Hoang, "It seems so different." But, what could I expect?

Alas, I began to comprehend that my Khe Sanh and my Vietnam now existed only in the history books—- and my diminishing memory. I later mentioned this feeling to Chaplin Ray Stubbe who pointed out that people who live in the past, as I suspect many vets do, dwell there alone.

Perhaps.

But my return to Khe Sanh did not grant me the liberating experience I so desperately sought. Instead, it left me confused and full of ambiguity as I struggled to come to terms with the reality of Khe Sanh in 1996.

I felt like walking around and perhaps locating some familiar landmarks, but Hoang declared adamantly that no one could go off the trail. Only a month earlier, a local villager had been killed by UXO as he dug in the ground no more than thirty yards from where we stood. Amazingly, many Vietnamese worked in the field digging and hoeing, seemingly inured to the dangers loitering beneath their feet. I later learned that several people died planting coffee on the old base.

Fortunately, my fellow travelers interrupted my reverie. An eclectic group of European young people crowded around me when one of the students asked if I had actually been at Khe Sanh during the battle. My reminiscing turned into a "History of the Siege of Khe Sanh class" as I pointed out the various landmarks and tried to explain what had occurred twenty-eight years earlier.

A young Irish woman asked me "was it bad?"

Yes.

A Dutch woman asked me if I felt strange being back here.

Yes.

Nevertheless, despite my efforts, I could not really express to a bunch of strangers what Khe Sanh meant to me. To them, I symbolized just another war relic, similar to the airstrip.

As I briefed the Europeans, I mentioned the persistent Khe Sanh fog. Just then, our guide yelled, "Here it comes." Sure enough, fog suddenly rolled in from the northwest and we understood that the time had come to depart. As we walked down the trail, I noticed a color television in a Vietnamese house in the village. A traveling companions pointed to the likelihood that they were watching "Little House on the Prairie," one of the most popular shows in Vietnam. Despite the poignancy of the moment, I laughed uproariously at the irony of it all. Did any greater proof exist of the utter futility of the Vietnam War?

Hardly anyone on the bus spoke on the long return trip to Hue as we drove down Highway One in the fading daylight. Out of the blue, I thought to move away from the window in case someone threw a grenade through it. My confrontation with the war had just begun and would not be resolved in one day or, maybe, a lifetime.

Khe Sanh 1997

When I returned to the DMZ area in 1997, the harsh aftermath of our extensive bombing campaign came home to me in stark terms. Rather than take a tour, I rented a car and driver in Hue and hired a guide/translator named Chi in Dong Ha.

At the old Camp Carroll, I discovered vast amounts of scrap metal left over from the war. Using homemade metal detectors, local Vietnamese dug up shell fragments to earn around twenty-five cents a day, despite the extreme danger of a round going off as they excavated for it. Chi told me that if they found a large bomb they could earn as much as $100 for detonating the old round in a lake to harvest fish.

Camp Carroll had an interesting history. When North Vietnam launched a cross-border invasion of South Vietnam in 1972, the South Vietnamese commander of Camp Carroll surrendered the position without a fight. As a reward for his treachery, the Communists made him a colonel in their army. In 2002, I found out that he ran a hotel in Hue. After repeated and torturous efforts to arrange an interview with him, I finally visited his home in 2003, but then I learned that he had recently suffered a stroke and could not speak. Nor would he allow me to interview his wife, but the luxury of his home and his obvious financial success said volumes about the price he earned for betraying his country. No doubt he fervently hopes that the Communists never lose power during his lifetime, for his neighbors might exact a terrible revenge on him for his wartime actions.

As we traveled towards Khe Sanh in 1997, the extreme heat and dryness of the region and the pronounced absence of trees surprised me. According to Chi, the U.S. dropped and/or sprayed 45,000 tons of napalm and defoliants along the DMZ during the war, so much firepower and herbicide that we actually changed the climate of central Vietnam. The area now exhibits a much drier and warmer environment than before because so much vegetation died under our aerial assault. Moreover, some researchers claim that it

Homemade metal detectors and UXO hunters at Camp Carroll (1997)

will take the Vietnamese ecosystem at least a century to recover from the effects of Agent Orange. To prevent erosion the local people have planted numerous Eucalyptus trees, as they were about the only foliage that could stand the increased heat of central Vietnam. Closer to the border with Laos, the environment seemed more vibrant when I observed miles and miles of banana trees on a later trip in 2003. But the plant life grew in soil heavily saturated with Agent Orange, which could be continuing the process of reintroducing dioxin into the Vietnamese food chain.

By 1997 Highway Nine had been upgraded considerably, and Khe Sanh town featured a large number of new homes. According to Chi, Hanoi believed that Highway Nine had great economic potential because it represented the shortest route to the ocean from Thailand and Laos. Thus, the Vietnamese government wanted to build an international highway connecting Thailand, Laos, and Burma to the port at Danang. The Vietnamese had rebuilt the municipality as well as part of a government program to re-settle Vietnamese in the mountains and dilute the influence of the local Highland tribes.

Yet, by 1997, the area's tourist potential had only begun to emerge. According to Chi, a mere 62 tourists visited the region in 1991. Within three years, 8,083 had explored the vicinity, and in 1996, more than 12,000 came to the place. Interestingly, Chi claimed that very few Americans had traveled to the vicinity by that time; most came from Europe and Japan. Indeed, my Khe Sanh tee shirt, which depicted battle scenes from 1968, sparked lots of positive comments from many Vietnamese when they realized that I was a returning American vet.

When I returned to Khe Sanh in 1997, I also found unexploded ammunition still scattered around the old base. Apparently many of the shells had migrated to the surface during the intervening years as the heat from the summer sun caused lots of explosions.

My guide, Chi, warned me, "If they start smoking, run." He really did not have to tell me that. Amusingly, in 1997, Chi told me that the Vietnamese government had not cleaned up the base yet because it wanted to promote tourism by retaining the authenticity

RAS area (Khe Sanh 1997)

PAVN memorial (Khe Sanh, 1997)

The author at Khe Sanh (1997)

of the battle site. Even when I visited Khe Sanh again in 2002, after the whole base had been converted into a coffee plantation, I almost stepped on a live round. My guide just about had a nervous breakdown as I laughed and tried to explain the irony of dying at Khe Sanh in the twenty-first century.

Danang 1997

I also revisited Danang in 1997 and found that the Vietnamese had converted the airfield where most of us arrived in South Vietnam into Danang International Airport. When I looked closely, I could still make out the tops of Quonset huts above the tree line, along with some of our old revetments. As I viewed the mountains that rose up closely to the west of Danang, a great sadness took hold of me when I reflected on all of the young, idealistic Americans who arrived here and walked into those hills, never to return to their families.

Often when I went to the Danang PX in 1968, I encountered South Korean (Republic of Korea or ROK) soldiers lingering by the door and asking people to purchase American cigarettes for them from the off-limits (to them) PX. I struggled to understand the logic in denying allied soldiers fighting and dying for our cause in South Vietnam access to our facilities. But, then again, the U.S. Air Force had the same stance towards the U.S. Marines who protected their airbase.

Danang International Airport (1997)

Nevertheless, I usually agreed to buy smokes for the Koreans out of a sense of allied solidarity and a dash of caution because of their nasty reputations. Indeed, by 1968, the South Koreans had become legendary in Vietnam as a result of their ferociousness and brutality towards the local population. In fact, when ROK convoys barreled down the highway, everyone—including my Marine driver—pulled over. This constituted really abnormal behavior for him, given that he believed that the best way to avoid being vaporized by a landmine was to drive so fast that it would detonate long after we had triggered it. But even he feared the ROK troops.

Nor did the South Koreans seem eager to shed their fierce status. Amazingly, years later a taxi driver picked me up in Iksan, South Korea, and greeted me in excellent English. When I asked him where he had learned the language, he told me that he had served with the ROK Tiger Brigade in Vietnam. At the same time, he made a motion with his hands like he was firing a machine gun. I said, "Man, you guys killed a lot of people." He responded, "We killed them all."

Few Americans appreciate the extent of ROK participation in the war. Over 300,000 South Korean soldiers supported the U.S. in the conflict; more than 5,000 died. The Korean War Memorial in Seoul dedicated an entire floor to their exploits in Vietnam, including a Viet Cong tunnel complex, complete with the sound of dripping water. ROK soldiers also suffered high rates of PTSD, and the continuing scourge of Agent Orange afflicted many of their children. Ironically, many Koreans believe that South Korean leader Park Chung Hee utilized the increased U.S. aid he received for sending his forces to the conflict to launch South Korea's startling economic growth in the 1970s and 1980s. However, one Korean lawyer pointed out to me that the money could not possibly compensate for the costs incurred by the South Korean government to recompense its veterans for their postwar ailments.

Despite the relative safety of the city in 1968, the local insurgents shelled the Danang airstrip on a regular basis. One morning after I returned from Rest and Relaxation (R&R) in Australia, I waited in an endlessly long line at the chow hall, a siren went off as a few incoming rounds shrieked in to impact on the base. One of the Marines jumped up and ran into the chow hall yelling, "Everyone out now!" After most of the personnel had fled to the safety of their bunkers, he turned to me and said, "Hey, Doc, you want an omelet?" We enjoyed a hearty breakfast, although several people glared at us when they returned after the "all clear" sounded.

Another evening, I dove underneath my cot in the transit tent, which the local command had inexplicably placed next to the runway, while enemy rockets exploded on the airstrip. The guy next to me asked if I had ever heard any stories about U.S. defectors serving with the Viet Cong. I said yes, because at that time rumors abounded about Americans who had joined the Communists in fighting us. The Marine claimed that he had been on patrol one day when a Caucasian walked into the middle of their formation as they took a break. Unexpectedly, someone yelled, "Hey, he's carrying an AK-47!" Apparently, the defector fled before anyone could cut him down. Years later, when I read about an American who had allegedly defected to the other side and then later learned that the U.S. had created a special unit to hunt down turncoats, I wondered who had really walked into that clearing that day.

In addition to beer, or because of it, I wanted to become better acquainted with ladies of a "friendly persuasion." Although South Vietnam gained a legendary reputation for the virulent sexually transmitted diseases that developed there in the midst of the colossal brothel culture that materialized during the war, most of us remained unconcerned about such mundane details. Indeed, when my opportunity arrived, I asked a Military Policeman (MP) on a street corner the best method for finding sociable women. He responded, "You are not supposed to ask me that, Doc, but just go down that street."

The next time I landed in the city I decided to search again for female companionship. A friendly Vietnamese taxi driver picked me up and, despite our language differences, understood what I wanted. When he stopped at the end of a driveway and gestured towards an alley at the end, I felt a little leery about the situation until a lovely young lady appeared and waved at me, so I assumed that everything must be okay. I walked to the passage and turned in the direction the woman had gone when I realized that I had entered a very narrow area with high walls on each side. I quick-ened my pace but when I reached the only door that I could see, I discovered it locked. At that point, I assumed that a grenade would come over the barrier so I slowly backed out with my body against the wall and my pistol drawn. By the time I reached the street again, my ardor had cooled considerably. To this day, I have no idea what happened to the woman who waved at me.

Danang seemed like a mean and angry place in 1968. The level of anti-Americanism among the South Vietnamese in the city shocked me. One afternoon, Vietnamese school girls on a local bus taunted me by expressing their preference for Ho Chi Minh, whom they considered "Number 1," as opposed to U.S. Marines, whom they deemed "number 10." In fact, over the years, many Vietnam-ese commented on the hot-tempered, ill-mannered reputation of many of the city's residents. Not much had changed by 1997.

Khe Sanh 2002

By 2002, Hanoi must have decided that killing foreigners would not enhance Vietnam's reputation as a tourist destination and thus had disposed of much of the UXO at the Khe Sanh base. In

2002, I also discovered that the Vietnamese had built a replica of one of our old bunkers and had constructed an interpretive center to commemorate the battle. One photo there showed scores of incoming rounds impacting on the base as it became consumed in the sea of fire that had been our precious ammunition.

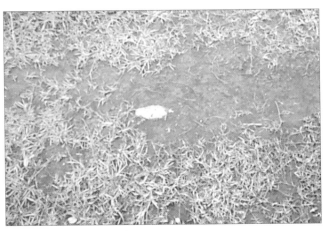

UXO (Khe Sanh, 2002)

Indeed, the DMZ had become an industry. Incredibly, my guide claimed that the Vietnamese government wanted to restore the Khe Sanh base, including the airstrip. I had to pay 25,000 dong ($1.66) for admission to the old base and had to hire a guide for twenty dollars (US) to enter the region.

Admission to Khe Sanh?

Some of the photos in the interpretive center carried hilarious captions. One alleged "encircled and attached intrepidly, the American soldiers lead their miserable lives at the base." Another declared, "The American and South Vietnamese units are rushing to the helicopters to run away from the Khe Sanh hell." One header incorrectly referred to the noted historian and President John F. Kennedy advisor Arthur Schlesinger Jr. as the Minister of War. I tried to explain to the museum curator and my guide that the U.S. does not have ministers in its government and that Schlesinger most likely wrote the exhibited letter as a private citizen, but I could not get anywhere with them.

By March 1968, Schlesinger had become so incensed with the shortcomings of Westmoreland's strategic thinking that he had written an emotional and provocative letter to the editor of the

Reconstructed bunker at Khe Sanh (2002)

Planter's house on our former runway (Khe Sanh, 2002)

Khe Sanh coffee farmers (2002)

Khe Sanh market (2002)

Khe Sanh interpretive center (2002)

Washington Post during the siege of Khe Sanh. In his letter, he argued, "There is a terrible irony about Khe Sanh. For the one elementary point, which everyone has made, since we first sent over combat units in 1965 has been that, whatever we do, we must not repeat the fatal error of the French and place a large body of troops out in the hills where they can be surrounded and cut off. Yet this is precisely what we have succeeded in doing at Khe Sanh." He pointed out that Khe Sanh had no military value but continued to be defended because "Khe Sanh is the bastion, not of the American military position, but of General Westmoreland's strategy—his 'war of attrition' which has been so tragic and spectacular a failure." Unfortunately, his failure left a many scars on both sides, as I discovered with alarming regularity after 1968.

Confronting the Lost Patrol

My efforts to come to terms with Khe Sanh also occurred in the U.S. During the summer of 1997, the Khe Sanh veterans held their reunion in St. Louis. One day, we visited Jefferson Barracks, which had two mass graves for men who died at Khe Sanh: one for eight men killed in the ambush whose bodies could never be identified, and another for forty-four men who were aboard an aircraft shot down by North Vietnamese anti-aircraft fire as it approached the base. The emotionally taxing and extremely sad memorial service stressed values like honor, courage, and sacrifice and left me with a sense of tremendous loss and awareness of the war's continuing impact on the people who fought in it.

After the memorial service, concluding that I had earned a well-deserved beer, I headed for the hotel tavern. When my wife and I walked in, two Khe Sanh vets already at the bar asked what I did at Khe Sanh. When they realized that I had been a corpsman, of course, they bought me a beer.

Over time, these two fellows came to epitomize for me the Vietnam War and its aftermath. One wore an eye patch, bore scars on his face, and had a cane hanging on the bar. He had been wounded at Khe Sanh, where he lost his eye, part of his face, and a portion of his leg. Astonishingly, despite his disability, he had stayed in the Marine Corps and had retired from the USMC. As he

Mass graves at Jefferson Barracks (St. Louis, 1997)

related his amazing story, I thought to myself, "God! What a man," in that he exemplified the audacious Marines I had admired throughout my lifetime.

Next to him sat a short fellow wearing utilities from top to bottom, which instantly made me suspicious, because so many Vietnam War wannabes wear camouflage to heighten the effect of their fictional accounts of Vietnam. But by the end of the conversation, I felt pretty convinced that he was for real. He claimed that he had been a member of the reaction force at Khe Sanh chosen to rescue the lost patrol. As we spoke, I sensed that he remained deeply troubled by the whole experience. He declared that he had a disability from the Veteran's administration for PTSD, and it seemed apparent that he had difficulty readjusting from the fighting. When the topic of the memorial service arose, he said over and over again, "You know we were ready to go get those guys. We were ready to go get those guys." While I recognized that our commanders had made the reasonable military decision not to send another force out after the lost patrol, which undoubtedly would have walked into the inevitable ambush that awaited them, it still represented an extraordinarily painful decision for everybody at Khe Sanh and had devastated the balance of his life.

Later that night, when we went back into the tavern to have a nightcap, we could not help but notice that the guy in the green utilities still sat at the bar. He seemed pretty drunk and I realized that every night of his life had likely unfolded the same way. He probably sat in some bar, with his utilities on, saying, "We were ready to go get those guys."

All of this occurred as I composed a doctoral dissertation about a peace movement in Vietnam. I tried to straddle both camps by going to a veteran's reunion with people who fought in the nastiest, bloodiest, meanest battle of the Vietnam War while at the same time reading materials about Vietnamese peace activists. Increasing my rather abundant bitterness, by that point, I had ascertained that the U.S. government knew as early as 1966 that it could not win the war and that the majority of the people in the Johnson administration wanted to get out of Vietnam. Probably more than anyone else, I realized that the young men we memorialized that day had died in a cause that our government had written off two years before the siege.

Tommy

At the same reunion, I encountered Tommy, a Khe Sanh vet who contacted me after I had written a letter to the editor of the Khe Sanh veteran's magazine calling into question the official—and fanciful—USMC casualty figures for the battle at Khe Sanh. Tommy had been seriously burned in a fire at the Khe Sanh ammo dump in 1968, but he had never received a Purple Heart for his wounds. In 1997, he wanted to demonstrate to the government that he actually had been injured so he could qualify for disability because of his Huntington's disease. Fortunately, through the efforts of Ray Stubbe and lots of other people, we finally persuaded the Marine Corps to give Tommy a Purple Heart.

I had been involved in the second dump explosion and could document the fact that an actual detonation had occurred as a result of enemy fire, which advanced Tommy's claim. But no evidence existed that proved that I had rescued him. Nevertheless, he spent all weekend buying me beer and introducing me to everyone as the corpsman who prolonged his earthly existence.

Interestingly, at the same reunion I ran into another severely wounded vet working at one of the PX tables. I told him that I had been a corpsman. Of course, given that he had served as a Marine, he loved corpsmen. But when I mentioned going back to Vietnam, he deemed the concept repellant. Regrettably, I pressed him on it until he looked me in the eye and said "Doc, I could never do that." When he turned on his heel and walked away, I noticed that he had a severe limp. Later on, my wife saw him by the swimming pool and she said he had deep scars on his legs. I remain sure that his physical disabilities reminded him every day of the war and the pain that it had caused him. Yet, I discovered over the next decade that such pain endured in Vietnam, as well.

PART II
THE VIETNAMESE

CHAPTER 6

Heroic History

"I don't like Ho Chi Minh."
-Vietnamese cyclo driver

Before embarking on the defense of Khe Sanh, Washington should have reviewed the long history of Vietnam's response to foreign invasion to gauge the possibility of Vietnamese timidity in the face of annihilation. In December 2000, while driving through the countryside in the Seven Mountains region of southern Vietnam, close to the Cambodian border, I came upon a beautiful, ornate temple in the midst of the rural poverty that encompasses much of modern Vietnam. The religious structure contained numerous depictions of Vietnamese history and heroes, including an altar to Ho Chi Minh and other defenders of Vietnam. Later that week, in Ho Chi Minh City, I stayed at a hotel on Cach Mang Thang Tam Street (August Revolution) which intersected Hai Ba Trung Street (the Trung sisters), and downtown I encountered a gigantic, menacing, and forceful statue of Tran Hung Dao, the Vietnamese general who routed the Mongols in the thirteenth century.

A walk through any Vietnamese city exposes one to the broad sweep of the country's history. These monuments also stand as poignant reminders that the Vietnamese define themselves in terms of their response to foreign invasion. While the Vietnamese revere courage, their worship of gallant figures from the past takes on practical aspects during times of crisis as they look back to their intrepid ancestors for inspiration to lead them to victory.

A continuity of thought concerning foreign interference weaves through thousands of years of Vietnam's history. Indeed, the Vietnamese reacted to Mongol, Chinese, French, and American incursions in remarkably similar ways, although the invasions occurred centuries apart. In every case, the Vietnamese looked to their past for motivation to regain or retain their independence. Hence, the U.S. war, coming after two thousand years of heroic history, appears exceptional only in the price paid by the Vietnamese to repel the Americans.

Army of the Republic of Vietnam (ARVN)

During the war, most Americans remained dangerously ignorant of Vietnam's heroic history. Many believed that South Vietnamese soldiers were incapable and unwilling to defend their own country. Nevertheless, the ARVN grew out of the same tradition that produced the ferocious and incredibly tough North Vietnamese who made our lives miserable at Khe Sanh. Certainly, the Vietnamese continued their tradition of resisting foreign invaders by fighting on both sides at Khe Sanh while the ARVN ultimately paid a heavy price for choosing to stand with us.

Ironically, the U.S. had been instrumental in building the South Vietnamese army, although we mainly trained and equipped it to repel a conventional Korean War-style cross-border invasion of South Vietnam. In other words, we assembled an almost completely conventional force that was uniquely unqualified to fight an insurgency despite Vietnam's long history of resorting to irregular warfare to defeat invaders. But the greatest irony of all must be that, in the end, South Vietnam fell to a conventional PAVN offensive in 1975.

Originally formed by the French to combat the Viet Minh, the ARVN developed under less than perfect circumstances given the extremely chaotic conditions in South Vietnam at the time of its formation in 1954. A bitter colonial war between France and the Viet Minh had recently ended in the partition of Vietnam along the seventeenth parallel. Devastated from years of turmoil and warfare, the country appeared to have little chance of surviving. Nevertheless, Washington remained deeply concerned over the possibility of an invasion of South Vietnam by the communist North Vietnamese and, thus, lavished weapons and military technology on South Vietnam. American military largess reached stunning proportions in the early years of South Vietnam and contributed substantially to the perception that South Vietnam merely constituted an American creation. In fact, American financial aid to South Vietnam in 1955 and 1956 accounted for 65 percent of the total budget of South Vietnam and 90 percent of the cost of maintaining ARVN.

By the time of the 1968 siege, U.S. press accounts of ARVN corruption and ineptitude had become so commonplace that South Vietnamese forces retained little credibility with their American allies. But, in the early years of the U.S. involvement in South Vietnam, Washington's propensity to use the ARVN as a vehicle to discard governments not to its liking had contributed to the endemic instability in South Vietnam and led to the introduction of U.S. ground forces. Indeed, from the time of the US-encouraged overthrow of President Ngo Dinh Diem by ARVN officers in 1963, until the ascension of another South Vietnamese officer, Prime Minister Nguyen Cao Ky, in 1965, ARVN generals engaged in almost constant intrigues to seize political power. Tragically, the U.S. eventually fought a war in which many members of the South Vietnamese military had seemingly lost interest. Moreover, from 1967 until the waning days of South Vietnam in 1975, another South Vietnamese general, Nguyen Van Thieu, ruled the country with an iron fist, rooting out domestic opposition and maintaining large numbers of troops around Saigon to guard against potential coups.

Yet, the U.S. had initially invited the ARVN to interfere with the civilian government of South Vietnam and then worsened the problem of ARVN ineffectiveness by inserting American combat forces, which further marginalized the South Vietnamese Army and relieved it from the duty of defending its own country. Thus, engaging in politics and leaving the fighting to the Americans became the primary occupation of a number of high-ranking South Vietnamese officers for the remainder of the war.

The inability of the South Vietnamese to create an effective fighting force arose from a number of factors. The racist paternalism demonstrated by the condescending attitudes of U.S. officials towards Vietnamese, particularly ARVN, and the blatant indifference towards Vietnamese lives and property exhibited by American forces aggravated an already touchy issue. Some Vietnamese found especially galling American stereotypes about Asians' ability to endure pain more stoically than Caucasians and the commonly held opinion that "life is cheap in East Asia." Many Vietnamese concluded that American racism drove the actions that served as such a potent recruiting tool for the Communists. At the same time, the use of napalm, defoliants, white phosphorous, cluster bombs, and

B-52 strikes seemed to confirm that American leaders wanted to eradicate a new yellow peril in Asia.

Vietnamese intellectuals particularly resented the way the American onslaught against traditional Vietnamese values had degraded the cultural fabric of the nation. To them, the role of Vietnamese women under the American cultural assault became especially charged and created enormous bitterness. Greed, increased consumerism, prostitution, and the disrespect shown married women enhanced South Vietnamese feelings of shame over their occupation by a foreign power. Adding to the humiliation felt by Vietnamese, ARVN troops never won the large battles or participated in the war in a meaningful way, and the spectacle of Vietnamese digging through American garbage dumps for food left an indelible impression on Vietnamese nationalists.

US officials looked upon elite South Vietnamese units as the backbone of the South Vietnamese army and the core around which an effective military organization could be fashioned. Even though the U.S. bore the major cost of training and equipping the ARVN, Saigon deployed South Vietnamese Marines in a failed attempt to liberate Danang from ARVN rebels in 1966, Vietnamese Rangers to break up demonstrations in Nha Trang, and South Vietnamese paratroopers to combat students in Saigon. The continued utilization of military forces to confront South Vietnamese civilians rather than the Viet Cong contributed to a further erosion of the combat capability of ARVN. The decline in South Vietnamese effectiveness also led to the introduction of more U.S. combat units utilizing increased firepower, which sparked greater manifestations of anti-Americanism and expanded civilian casualties.

Although Washington claimed to support the restoration of a non-military regime, it constantly asserted that the South Vietnamese army remained the only force able to hold the country together and carry the fight to the Communists. In spite of that, ARVN represented an extremely unsettling force with its constant intrigues, bullying of civilian administrators, and propensity to overthrow governments. Certainly, the primary function of ARVN became the control of the restive populace of South Vietnam, not protecting the people from the Communist menace. At the same time, the people the army had been charged to protect suffered even more under the American military offensive.

American insensitivity went far beyond an irresponsible use of firepower. Depredations against Vietnamese civilians went beyond collateral damage. Numerous cases of U.S. Marines sexually molest-ing Vietnamese women, physically assaulting other civilians, caus-ing property damage during off-duty hours, and committing various other actions led Marine commanders to create a Backlash Report to gauge reaction to incidents among the local populace. Although the USMC went to great lengths to indoctrinate its troops about the importance of maintaining good relations with civilians, the prevalent Marine culture that decreed that men who came out of the field usually got roaring drunk and raised hell until arrested, the inability to control Marines coming out of combat, the impact of men living in a state of constant fear, and the racism that afflicted most American soldiers in Vietnam overwhelmed efforts to im-prove relations with the Vietnamese. On top of that, Marines who came to Danang from the contested areas, appalled by the opulence of rear-echelon living conditions compared to the dismal conditions in the field, usually aimed their resentment at the people least responsible for their plight and least able to fight back: Vietnamese civilians. The problem for Marine officers could be best expressed by the familiar combat Marine expression: "What are they going to do, cut my hair off and send me to the Nam?" For many men, even time in the brig seemed preferable to life in the field.

ARVN Rangers

I formed my first impressions of South Vietnamese soldiers at Khe Sanh in 1968, when Westmoreland sent the 37th ARVN Ranger Battalion to the base to aid in its defense. We had so little confi-dence in South Vietnamese military abilities that Marine command-ers ordered them to construct their bunkers in front of our lines so that the Rangers solely guarded no part of our perimeter. How-ever, some commentators later argued that the ARVN took the positions outside of our lines to reinforce the most likely avenues of a PAVN attack and to add more guns to the defense of one end of the absolutely critical airstrip.

Many of us suspected that the South Vietnamese soldiers slept on watch at night because every morning we heard heavy firing from their lines. We assumed that they discharged their weapons to rouse their comrades, but it may have been because their positions sat closest to the North Vietnamese, who bur-rowed towards them every night. Thus, they fired to clear out any enemy soldiers who might have been sitting in the fog right outside of their bunkers.

Few of us would have believed that at the time. After treating at least a half-dozen of them for self-inflicted gunshot wounds, I concluded that they did not have their hearts in the war. Many of my early notions grew from that experience, but when I look back on it, their actions made sense, because to them, the war might go on forever. They did not serve a one-year or a thirteen-month tour like we did and, anyway, we did not want to be there either. Our dim view of our allies also ignored the fact that, according to political scientist James Anthony Joes, over 200,000 ARVN died fighting the Communists from 1954 to 1975, another 400,000 South Vietnamese suffered imprisonment when the Communists overran their country in 1975, the VCP executed some 65,000 former officials and soldiers after liberation, and another 200,000 South Vietnamese died in prison following the collapse of South Vietnam. (James Anthony Joes, *The War for South Vietnam*, 155).

When I returned to Vietnam decades after the fall of Saigon, my hostility and ambivalence towards the ARVN seemed terribly misplaced. At times during the war, particularly when defending their home areas, South Vietnamese units fought very well, but poor leadership, massive corruption, and inept national governments plagued them throughout the war. In fact, some historians argue that by pushing the South Vietnamese out of the way and Americanizing the conflict, the U.S. created the conditions that led to its defeat in Vietnam. The ARVN also suffered from a general lack of discipline in the ranks, numerous instances of extortion and crimes of violence against civilians, and almost non-existent morale.

Moreover, South Vietnamese generals became legendary for the staggering amounts of money they embezzled and the phony armies they created to get their share of American appropriations. Some quietly created truces with local insurgents so that the Communists could operate in an area without ever running into the ARVN. In some cases, they actually sold their US-supplied equipment to the Communists. Ironically, many corrupt South Vietnamese leaders successfully fled the country in 1975, leaving their desperate subordinates behind to bear the brunt of Communist reprisals.

In many ways, our negative attitudes towards ARVN grew out of the racist nature of our training. Marine instructors constantly harangued us on the importance of winning hearts and minds, but we never really listened to their opinions, despite the fact that their outlook could have helped us a lot. One instructor

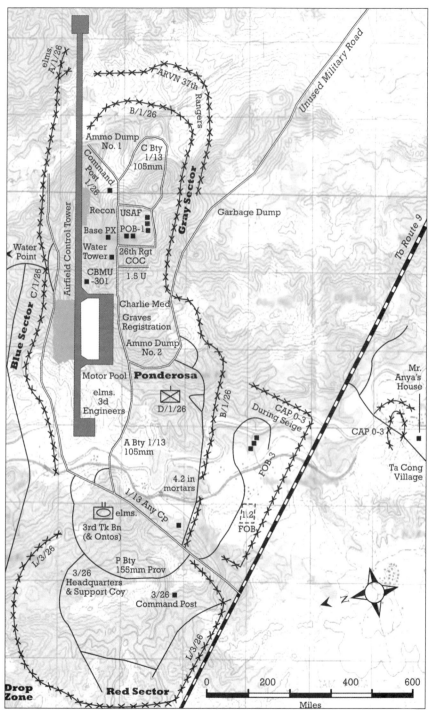

Map of base showing ARVN lines—Khe Sanh, 1968

assured us "Charlie (the Viet Cong) can't shoot straight," a statement that seemed less than reassuring when snipers drove us underground at Khe Sanh.

Our pre-combat training encouraged us to doubt Vietnamese abilities on many levels. During our prewar indoctrination, one sergeant bellowed, "When you walk into a South Vietnamese village and some old lady offers you a bowl of rice that's full of rat turds, you'll eat it anyway, because we're there to win the hearts and minds of these people!" That repelled us so much that we drew many absolutely wrong conclusions about the Vietnamese. They appeared to be a primitive people unable to engage in the simplest kind of human activity or sanitation. In truth, the Vietnamese traced their lineage back several thousand years and had created a rich and distinctive civilization.

Stories about South Vietnamese children selling bottles of cola with ground-up glass inside and launching terrorist attacks against Americans heightened our hostility and distrust of the Vietnamese. At the same time, the fact that many South Vietnamese soldiers held hands while walking together flew in the face of USMC hyper-masculinity and raised even more questions about our allies. Although we received stern lectures about offenses like defecating on Buddhist statues in pagodas or offering our cigarette lighters to Buddhist monks, we really did not care. (From 1963 to 1975, over seventy Buddhist monks and nuns set themselves afire in South Vietnam to protest against the war. Ironically, I later wrote the first English language book on the Buddhist peace movement). We mainly wanted to stay alive and remained so influenced by racist stereotypes of Asians that we barely considered them human beings. This became the major American problem in Vietnam: we so dehumanized the Vietnamese that their lives became unimportant to us even though we needed their loyalty to prevail against the Communists. But on a more basic level most of us developed a sense of racial superiority towards the South Vietnamese and the ARVN, in particular, which further demeaned them in our eyes.

Given that the ARVN position stood close to our aid station, we treated almost all of their casualties, many of which resulted from American forces. Often, nervous Marines shot ARVN when they awoke in the morning and stretched or when they moved around at night. One evening a tall ARVN officer arrived at our facility with a huge open wound across his back that, he claimed, had occurred when a trigger-happy Marine opened up on him as he checked on his troops. His height and excellent English made us extraordinarily jumpy because in the days before the siege, Marine sentries had killed several PAVN officers as they reconnoitered our lines. The rumor mill speculated that they had actually been Red Chinese officers assisting or directing the upcoming battle.

Thus, through a combination of racism, fear, and lunacy we became convinced that we had a potential double agent lying on the stretcher in front of us. Fortunately, our fears did not come true, although we probably should have asked ourselves about the logic of an enemy soldier exposing himself to potential deadly fire to infiltrate a medical facility. In the end, we patched him up as well and as quickly as we could and shipped him to Charlie Med. We also notified the command bunker about our suspicions. They are still probably laughing about it.

The ARVN medic often visited our aid station. I considered him a very competent individual who found himself constantly short on supplies, probably due to the same corruption that crippled the South Vietnamese army. However, the Vietnamese are nothing if not practical, so he traded war booty with me for medical provisions. At one point, he gave me a PAVN belt and a North Vietnamese gas mask and goggles that I later swapped for goods in Danang. He also offered me a piece of North Vietnamese currency with two bullet holes in it that he had taken off a dead, female North Vietnamese medic. Unfortunately, in my

North Vietnamese currency—Khe Sanh, 1968

discourse with him, I often referred to PAVN soldiers as gooks, not realizing that they were all Vietnamese and that my racist rhetoric negated his humanity as much as that of our enemies and myself.

Even though everyone suffered at Khe Sanh, the misery of the South Vietnamese seemed especially acute. Jimmy (our other corpsman) and I went down to the ARVN lines one day to deliver some medical supplies. As we walked though the area, Jimmy tripped over a claymore mine that easily could have detonated and killed us. But given that we inhabited Khe Sanh, we laughed like crazy because it seemed so funny, although it could have been so deadly. We also encountered the absolutely horrific and unsanitary living conditions of the South Vietnamese bunkers that reminded us that infectious disease could attack as effectively as the PAVN.

Indeed, the highly noxious condition of the base contributed to the outbreak of a frightening disease. One day an ARVN soldier walked into the aid station and pointed to a large boil in his groin area. I poked around the lesion and then asked the doctor to check it out. He walked into the room, took one glance at the sore, and said, "Oh, that looks like the plague."

Bubonic Plague?

The infamous Black Death?

The same disease that wiped out a large segment of Europe in the Middle Ages?

Did we need any further confirmation that we had entered into our own special nightmare from which there could be no escape?

We immediately drew a tissue sample and hustled it down to Danang. Sure enough, he had the Bubonic Plague, no doubt because of the rats overrunning our base, especially in the South Vietnamese sector, where they fed on the dead bodies on our wire. We had plague booster rushed to us and tried to administer a shot to every person on the base. In fact, we stayed up much of the night drawing the vaccine into syringes for our mass inoculation scheduled for the next day.

Subsequently, numerous Marines came to our aid station, where we administered the injections that we hoped might prevent an epidemic. When one Marine walked into the RAS, I was so tired because we had been up all night that I just swabbed his arm and gave him a shot. He turned and looked at me and said, "I'm not here for a shot. I already had one." We found his response absolutely hilarious.

One day while walking through the Recon area, I noticed a South Vietnamese soldier staked to the ground. That seemed extremely foolhardy given that Recon sat next to the airstrip and received more incoming than anyone else. When I inquired about the situation, one Marine claimed that he had found the ARVN Ranger stealing so he wanted to teach him a lesson by exposing him to PAVN fire.

His statement illustrated the racism that drove so much of what we did in Vietnam. Many South Vietnamese troops lacked food and supplies and often did not get paid. Despite the fact that the ARVN repelled a number of North Vietnamese probes and engaged in plenty of ground fighting at the base, they still received second-class treatment from their American allies. Moreover, many ARVN lost family members during the Tet Offensive when insurgents hit their home area particularly hard. They found themselves trapped at Khe Sanh, not knowing whether their domiciles had been overrun and perhaps their family members killed.

And we treated them as inferiors.

None of us recognized at that point that their problems had just begun. After the North Vietnamese conquered Saigon in 1975, the South Vietnamese suffered horribly at the hands of the Vietnamese Communist Party (VCP). Indeed, of all the tragic loose ends left over from the hostilities, the fate of former South Vietnamese soldiers represented one of the most heartbreaking and pitiful reminders of our Vietnam experience.

Conversations with ARVN

In December 2001, American Secretary of Defense Donald Rumsfeld publicly assured the Afghan people, in the midst of the war on terror, that the U.S. would always remain by their side, while accentuating Washington's commitment to a long-term relationship with Afghanistan. His statement struck me as stunningly ironic and cynical given that our former South Vietnamese allies have endured decades of withering persecution principally because of their wartime alliance with the U.S. Indeed, no one who visits postwar Vietnam can deny the retribution visited on former South Vietnamese officials and soldiers by the triumphant Communists after 1975.

Like many other veterans, I often felt that I had given a lot to my nation and received very little in return. Yet, at least I have had a country. After 1975, the ex-ARVN had no homeland, no pensions

and no grateful nation to celebrate their valor, only the sad realization that when their side lost, their safety net unraveled. Thus, they
experienced lives of terrible desolation as they struggled to survive
in a country ruled by a government that considered them non-
persons and rejected their very existence.

Many American veterans felt hostility towards the Vietnamese
after the war and hated them in a variety of ways. So did I, but
when I decided to write a master's thesis on the Buddhist Crisis of
1963 at Central Washington University in the early 1990s, I felt
impelled to conduct a number of interviews among the large
Vietnamese community in Seattle. Eventually, I visited a Vietnamese Buddhist temple in Olympia and got to know many of the
members of the pagoda, who treated me with genuine kindness
and offered to help me out in any way they could. Thereafter, my
perceptions of the Vietnamese evolved from my wartime outlook
that the Vietnamese all hated us to a more nuanced understanding
of their attitudes towards American veterans.

In 1995, I attended the University of Wisconsin to study
Vietnamese language and culture as one of the requirements for my
Ph.D. The large number of Viet Kieu (overseas Vietnamese) students attending the language course accelerated the process of
reevaluating my relationship with the Vietnamese. Over time, I
noticed that of the many of the Viet Kieu hung around me, leading
me to discover that, rather than hating us, many young Vietnamese
Americans admired and looked up to Vietnam veterans because
they believed that we fought to defend their home country. The
situation in Vietnam appeared to be similar: after many years under
Communism, most people in southern Vietnam had a high regard
for Americans and appreciated what we tried to do in their country. Even if our aims seemed misguided and caused an unacceptable level of destruction to the cultural fabric of South Vietnam,
they realized that had we won they might have avoided years of
Communist terror.

In fact, at one point, one of the young women in the program
invited me to stay at her house in San Francisco while I conducted
research in Berkeley. I slept on a futon in her living room where
she would sit on the floor every evening and talk to me about
Vietnam. Tragically, after the war, many Vietnamese did not
identify themselves as Vietnamese to Americans because so much
hostility arose towards the Vietnamese immigrants in the United
States.

Yet, the starkest evidence of Communist hostility towards ARVN appeared in Vietnam in 1975 when the Vietnamese government incarcerated most ARVN officers in a series of concentration camps the regime euphemistically called reeducation camps. Upon their release, after the VCP denied them the necessary documentation to gain regular employment. Hence, our former allies had to fend for themselves in an economy already suffering from severe unemployment. By 1996, many ex-South Vietnamese soldiers in Ho Chi Minh City drove cyclos—a three-wheeled bicycle-like contraption where the rider sat in front while the driver pedaled from behind—as part of the large informal and unregulated economy that sprang up in Vietnam as tourists began to visit the country in the 1990s. Ironically, their ability to speak English allowed many former South Vietnamese soldiers to eke out a living working with tourists after decades of despicable VCP persecution. When I traveled to Vietnam, cyclo drivers often approached me on the street and inquired about my nationality. As soon as they heard me say Hoa Ky (the United States), I found myself inundated by men who desperately wanted to acquaint me with their stories, show me their old wounds, tell me about their former outfits, mention that Hoa Ky still remained Number One, and ask if, by chance, I knew their American friends. Many also laid a major guilt trip on me in a sometimes-successful effort to have me compensate them for their postwar misery. In recent years, numerous younger Vietnamese pointed out how much their parents suffered because of their former association with the U.S. in a totally vain attempt to plead for reparations.

In 1996, a former ARVN soldier became my cyclo driver in Ho Chi Minh City for a week. Like most Saigonese, he seemed friendly, helpful, protective, and genuinely interested in assisting my research. After our third day together, he brought me a picture of his wife and started to buy me fruit whenever we traveled. One day, after he picked me up at the former presidential palace of Nguyen Van Thieu, he leaned over and whispered in my ear, "I don't like Ho Chi Minh."

Yet the war and its aftermath can never be far from his consciousness. He still had his reeducation camp identification number tattooed on his arm and, even more disturbing, he had no trigger finger. Eventually, I pointed to it and said "Cong San" (Communist), and he nodded his head yes. As time went on, I noticed more and more cyclo drivers appeared to be missing their trigger fingers.

In fact, one ex-ARVN greeted me by rubbing the stump of his absent digit into my hand and then simply refusing to let me go. After freeing myself from his iron grip, I decided to forgo any further investigation on the subject that day and headed for the hotel bar.

I never discovered any evidence that the VCP systematically mutilated ARVN vets, so I was left with many more questions over this issue than answers. I surmised that the Communists may had hacked off their fingers to guarantee that they would never fight again, or possibly the veterans inflicted the wounds on themselves to assuage the fears of the party. Or maybe it was just a coincidence. But, it served as a poignant reminder of the price they paid for serving the interests of the U.S. even though many Americans now acknowledge our misguided aims in Vietnam. Yet, many of the former ARVN still believed in the United States with almost a childlike faith in its goodness and benevolence. No doubt, they also wished that 500,000 nineteen-year-olds would come back and again lavish money on their country and, in some ways, they finally got their wish. In 2003, the U.S. Navy made its first postwar port-call at Saigon Harbor as part of the continuing thaw in US-Vietnamese relations.

Nevertheless, some or our ex-allies remained so desperate for money that they would beseech me to let them take me anywhere. Often, even if I only had a short walk in mind, they persisted, and after a while their pleading became particularly unnerving because I knew that they would likely go hungry if they did not get a fare. The farther north I went, the more this situation arose, no doubt reflecting the fact that Saigon had regained its status as the engine that drove the Vietnamese economy.

My first day in Hue, as I walked down Le Loi Street to find a school attended by Ho Chi Minh, cyclo drivers accosted me, demanding that I use their conveyance. I tried to make it clear that I really did not need a ride and increased my stride to avoid their entreaties. Even when I went jogging, cyclo drivers pleaded with me to ride in their vehicles. During my later trips, I discovered that walking on the same side of the street as a police station or an army base remained the best way to avoid relentless cyclo drivers. None dared risk a confrontation with the dreaded security services and, thus, they generally left me alone.

In 1997, I took a shuttle van from Hue to Danang. As it turned out, the driver had served in a South Vietnamese Airborne unit, had been wounded three times during the conflict, and still carried a bullet in his back. He claimed that an American doctor had saved him. The moment he found out that I had been a corpsman, he started calling me "Doc." As we drove through Hue, he kept pulling over the van and introducing me to different people, pointing to me as an American who had revisited Vietnam.

As we moved down the road, I recorded our conversation in my notebook. Suddenly, a horrified look swept across his face. He implored, "Please don't use my name!" When I scratched it out and showed him that I had blanked it out of my notes, he thanked me profusely, claiming that after his release from reeducation, the Communists would not give him papers to secure work. Like so many of our former associates, despite having to support a wife and four children, he could not obtain employment for close to twenty years until the growing tourist industry enabled him to find a job where he could utilize his English skills.

At one point, as we drove over Hai Van Pass—the most beautiful place on earth, where the rice paddies meet the sea—he looked at me and said, "You know, we are lucky to be alive," a statement that I have heard from many former North and South Vietnamese soldiers. Interestingly, the last time I had been on Hai Van Pass in 1968, an American fighter jet roared overhead and launched rockets against a suspected enemy position on the hillside as I sleepily admired the scenery from the back of a truck.

Hai Van pass—2002

At the top of the mountain, one can gain a sense of modern Vietnamese history by observing the French, American, and Vietnamese Imperial bunkers that dot the hillsides.

The next day in Danang, an old man who spoke English with a French accent approached me, introduced himself as Mr. Hai, and offered his services as a translator. He had worked for the U.S. for fifteen years as an interpreter and insisted rather stridently that the Americans still owed him a month's pay, probably for April 1975. When I asked if he went to reeducation, he assured me "But of course," a response heard way too often from our previous allies. He spent two years being "reeducated" but then, upon his return, he could not secure regular employment until the explosion of tourism in the 1990s created new opportunities for him.

He agreed to take me on his motorcycle for the rest of the day and to provide me a car and driver the next day. After his motorcycle kept stalling, I suggested that we try again at another time, but he insisted that we continue, no doubt so that he could collect a half-day's pay. He took me across the Danang River Bridge and then south towards Marble Mountain, where he showed me the one-time III MAF Headquarters and the old ammo dump.

After stopping briefly to take a picture, we started to pull away from the curb when suddenly his hat flew off. I jumped off to retrieve it, but he just kept going, unaware that a passenger no

Mr. Hai—Danang, 1997

longer sat on his motorcycle. I looked up and saw him blissfully speeding away. I hitched a ride back to town and stopped at a cool restaurant/bar alongside the river. Amazingly, when I came out after several beers, Mr. Hai stood there battered and bruised from a run-in with a drunk driver but, nonetheless, eager to work the next day.

Hieu

One way or another, some people found a way to survive in postwar Vietnam. In 1999, I met a former South Vietnamese soldier and present-day motorcycle driver in Ho Chi Minh City named Hieu. He lost an eye during the war, but he did not get sent to reeducation. Instead, the new regime kicked his family out of Saigon because the Communists wanted to reduce the city's war-time population explosion. Indeed, Saigon grew from a city of 1.4 million in 1962 to 2.5 million in 1965 to 4.5 million by mid-1967. By August 1967, *25 percent* (my italics) of the population of South Vietnam resided in the Saigon area.

Hieu worked in the countryside for two years and then slipped back into the city to find work. He eventually became my favorite motorcycle driver and my semi-permanent driver. Several times we drank beer together while he related his wartime experiences and the difficulties he encountered after the conflict. For the first few years after he returned to Saigon, he worked as a cyclo driver because he spoke English, but eventually, he saved enough money to buy a motorcycle. Most days he only made about a dollar

Hieu—Ho Chi Minh City, 2002

and a half, which explained why he always seemed so pleased to see me.

But his half-blindness presented a number of problems especially in an urban area the size of Ho Chi Minh City that had an unofficial population of some seven million people by the end of the twentieth century with 90 percent of the city's residents driving motorcycles. Not surprisingly, riding through the city with a one-eyed driver as over five million motorcycles coursed around the metropolis proved interesting. I constantly held up my hand to prevent other cyclists from crashing into us.

Yet, despite the travail endured by Hieu and other ex-ARVN, I also detected numerous examples of VCP retribution aimed not simply at former supporters of the Saigon regime but at anyone who represented a potential threat to the government.

CHAPTER 7

Dissidents

"She was born in Ho Chi Minh City, but I was born in Saigon."
- Saigon bartender, 2005

One evening in 1997, as I drank beer in the DMZ Bar and Café (what genius thought that name up?) in Hue, the son of a former ARVN officer who fled to France after the war introduced himself to me.

DMZ bar—Hue 2003

Like so many other former South Vietnamese, he was—and probably still is—rabidly anti-Communist. At one point, while we drove through the city on his motorcycle, he stopped and introduced me to his children. When we got back on his bike, I quipped,

"So, how do your children like living in this socialist paradise?" He dissolved into bitter laughter. But he had not left his homeland like countless other Vietnamese because he worried about maintaining the graves of his ancestors. With his father gone, that solemn responsibility had fallen on his shoulders. Indeed, the Vietnamese believe deeply in kin and ancestry, and many experienced severe emotional anguish when they left their family graves behind and migrated to the United States or other venues to escape Communism.

Loc and his kids—Hue, 1997

Shortly afterward, the police detained him. At that time, Vietnamese law forbade private citizens from transporting tourists or foreigners without a permit. Hanoi also disallowed aliens from staying in Vietnamese homes without registering with the government. In fact, Vietnamese hotels required guests to turn over their passports, so that the clerks could register their names with the police. One monk claimed that the Cong An (the Communist police) maintained agents in all hotels to keep an eye on outsiders.

After the police officer signaled him to halt, my guide quickly instructed me, "Just get off the motorcycle and start walking. Let's meet somewhere else, later." I hurriedly strolled away and acted like a tourist. When we linked up afterward he claimed that his illicit act might carry a fine of as much as two hundred dollars—a princely sum in Vietnam. We agreed to bribe the cop and ended up negotiating a ten-dollar kickback, which for the police officer represented a lot of money. But avoiding arrest on that trip remained far more important to me.

My guides actions also indicated how many Vietnamese absolutely hate, loathe and detest the Communist Party of Vietnam for its reprehensible actions during and after the war. When southern Vietnamese found out my nationality, they often launched into wild denunciations of the Communists. One night, after a Vietnamese taxi driver discovered my country of origin, he ranted and raved about the Communists throughout the whole trip because they had killed his father during the war. Another former South Vietnamese told me that she had been forced out of Saigon after 1975, only to slip back into the city to operate a business clandestinely. Sadly, two of her sisters and her mother died while trying to escape Vietnam as boat people. In the midst of our conversation, she looked over at a young person and said with obvious pride, "She was born in Ho Chi Minh City, but I was born in Saigon." I kissed her on the forehead so that she would know that at least one American understood her pain.

Several years ago at an Internet café in Hoi An, I noted a picture of an ex-ARVN combatant hanging on the wall, which surprised me because former South Vietnamese soldiers remained non-people in Vietnam. After the owner identified the person in the photo as his father, he became very emotional and strident, talking about the dad he never knew and how the Communists had killed him. Anyone could have reported him for his outspoken criticism of the government, and he could have received a jail term for his outburst, but in the midst of his rage, he seemed unconcerned.

The next day, on a bus from Hoi An to Hue, a former South Vietnamese major and his new wife sat across from me. Providentially for him, he had been in Nha Trang (on the south central coast of Vietnam) in 1975 when South Vietnam fell to the Communists, and a navy friend helped him flee the country. When the South Vietnamese reopened the base at Khe Sanh to launch their disastrous 1971 invasion of Laos, he received several serious wounds during the operation.

He had come back to Vietnam to find a second mate after his first spouse had divorced him in the United States. In recent years, many former South Vietnamese soldiers and Viet Kieu (overseas Vietnamese) returned to Vietnam in search of wives because they wanted what they believed would be traditional women, but also because their incredible wealth compared to the average Vietnamese allowed them to easily locate new companions. Despite their newfound prosperity, most conveyed a deep melancholy that they had lost their country to the Communists. Sadly, for many of the South Vietnamese who fled to America in 1975, their Diaspora represented the second time the Communists had forced them from their homes. Indeed, close to one million Vietnamese escaped from North Vietnam in 1954 when the VCP came to power only to reestablish themselves in the south and be driven out again in 1975.

In 2003, I met a Vietnamese American on a flight to Hue who had been in the city in 1968. Although he was a small child at the time, he told me that he and his terrified family huddled in their basement for days as the fighting raged all around them. After the war, his family suffered expulsion from the city as the victorious Communists forced many city-dwellers to engage in agriculture. Hunger and Communist oppression finally led him to flee from the country to the US, where he became a software engineer. He and his wife had just returned to Vietnam to seek investment opportunities with the money he made during the Internet Technology (IT) revolution of the 1990s. In typical Vietnamese fashion, when he found out that I had come to Vietnam to help children suffering from Agent Orange he insisted that his brother-in-law—a taxi driver—take me to my hotel free of charge.

Not surprisingly, Vietnamese/Americans may be the most fervently anti-Communist people in America—or possibly even in the world—but they do not stand alone. (Many Cuban-Americans would disagree with me). One day as I jogged in a Ho Chi Minh City park wearing a U.S. Marine Corps tank top, an old man saluted me, letting me know in his way that he still appreciated the Marine Corps and Americans. In recent years, another former South Vietnamese hijacked an aircraft in Thailand with the intention of dropping anti-government leaflets over Vietnam. After his release from a Thai prison, the Vietnamese government insisted that he be extradited to Vietnam even though he had retained American citizenship. A different South Vietnamese drove a bull-dozer into the Vietnamese Embassy in Paris and planted a South Vietnamese flag on the grounds. He got the hell beat out of him by the legation guards but became an international hero to Vietnamese expatriates around the world.

Religious Freedom in Vietnam?

Vietnamese law enforcement created even more problems for me in 1997. As I entered Danang for the first time since 1968, the police pulled me over almost instantly merely because I was a foreigner and, thus, an easy mark. The cop demanded 20,000 dong ($1.50) to cover my "fine," and I quickly learned the language of corruption in Southeast Asia. My favorite phrase when confronted by the police became: "I am so sorry. Is there a fine I can pay so that I can be on my way?" Somehow we always settled our disputes without going to the police station.

A similar experience greeted me in Laos in 2004, while conducting research on the Hmong people, who suffered deeply at the hands of the Lao Communists after the U.S. withdrew its support in 1973. A hilltop police patrol pulled over our car as we entered the traditional Hmong homeland. Regrettably, my driver had allowed one of his licenses to expire, which rendered us particularly vulnerable to law-enforcement intimidation. As my two associates negotiated with the police, I lingered in the back of the car taking notes and trying to remain inconspicuous.

A sharp tapping sound on the window drew my attention to a cop who questioned what I was doing in his country. At that moment, I asked myself the same thing, especially because—and this really unnerved me—the Communist police in Laos wore the same uniforms as the Cong An in Vietnam. I gave him a guarded answer and offered him my business card. He carefully examined it before returning it with a crisp salute. The dialogue between the cops and my driver dragged on for some time until I stepped out of the car and asked the four police officers, "Can I take your picture?" Within minutes we were speeding down the road after my guide slipped a wad of money under the logbook on which his driver's license sat.

Like their Lao cousins, the Vietnamese police regularly shook down foreign visitors for bribes when the country first opened up to tourism in the early 1990s, but the practice became less common after the VCP realized that many tourists would go elsewhere rather than pay off the police. Once the word got out, many Cong An went out of their way to avoid speaking to Westerners for fear that they would be suspected of corruption. Once, when my driver stopped on a bridge over the Mekong River for me to take a photo, a cop pulled up and started to write him a ticket until he saw my Caucasian face and then abruptly waved us on. My driver, for his part, could not believe his good fortune, given that many Vietnamese view bribes as part of their everyday interactions with the authorities.

Early on, the Viet Kieu experienced especially vigorous Cong An efforts to extract pay-offs. In the mid-1990s, Vietnamese/ Americans commonly placed cash inside their passports to speed their way through Vietnamese customs. When one stubborn Viet Kieu refused to buy off the immigration cops at the Ho Chi Minh City airport in 1997, the police kept sending him back to the end of the line. Although I felt sorry for him, I decided to take advantage of my good fortune and get out of the airport before incurring another "fine." Corruption remained a serious issue in Vietnam, but the VCP ultimately adopted a much more thorough and systematic looting of the country through the high-level robbery of the people's assets rather than the simple shakedowns that the Vietnamese endure on a regular basis.

After the cop in Danang released me in 1997, my driver dropped me at my hotel and cautioned me, "Be careful at night in Danang. Walk in the lights." Apparently Danang suffered from a significant crime problem, but my main concern revolved around an article I had published the month before in a Vietnamese-language journal in Paris. My essay had severely disparaged the VCP, arguing that religious repression in Vietnam remained far more subtle and insidious than most Americans believed and maintained that the Communists' most pernicious action may have been the brutal anti-religious pogrom they launched after South Vietnam's collapse in 1975.

I had followed a long and winding path to that article. Eight months earlier in July 1996, at the An Quang pagoda in Ho Chi Minh City, headquarters of the militant Buddhists in the 1960s and afterward, I had attempted to contact Thich Tri Quang. The leader of the radical Buddhist faction during the war and the central figure of my book on the Buddhist peace movement, he had been under government restrictions for decades. I hoped that my unannounced appearance at the pagoda would prevent the police from observing or interrupting our meeting and encourage him to consent to an interview.

When I arrived, a monk directed me upstairs where a group of prelates chanted before an altar. No one seemed aware of my presence when, suddenly, an older cleric entered the room, sat next to another monk, slipped him something from underneath his robes, and then quickly left. At the same time, a young man on the balcony above the sanctuary bent over and tried to observe the actions below. Given that he might have been one of the many informers the Vietnamese government used to keep an eye on the remnants of the outlawed Unified Buddhist Church (UBC), the possibility of being swept up in a police raid arose in my mind. Indeed, I had already conducted a number of ostensibly illegal interviews because of my entry into the country on a tourist visa rather than the research document required by Vietnamese law.

Hence, I quickly left, but when I returned later, a monk told me that Thich Tri Quang never accepted visitors. My frequent endeavors to contact the Buddhist leader over the years had all failed; other Americans who had attempted to converse with the holy man had the same experience. At one point, as I passed within a few feet of Thich Tri Quang's door, a monk bent towards me and whispered "Confidentially, I think he is afraid of having more trouble with the government."

Having failed in my main quest, other seemingly less contro-versial, research opportunities beckoned. In March 1965, a number of spontaneous peace movements emerged in Saigon, no small feat in view of the fact that calling for neutralism— and later peace— represented a severe breach of South Vietnamese law. To the amazement and consternation of the South Vietnamese generals who ran the country, the antiwar efforts gained widespread accep-tance and backing. Unfortunately, some of the citizens who had signed a petition supporting the movement discovered that their "republic" planned to expel them from South Vietnam for calling for peace in the midst of an increasingly unpopular conflict. At first, the generals announced a plan to toss the offending parties out of a plane over Hanoi but eventually decided merely to escort them to the DMZ and send them to the other side of the bridge spanning the Ben Hai River.

A well known, Yale-educated Buddhist prelate, Thich Quang Lien, instigated one of the 1965 antiwar factions, which led to his temporary ouster from the country. We met in 1996, and in the course of our conversation, he asked my views on religious liberty in Vietnam. I initially gave him a non-committal answer, but when he asked me to speak freely, he received my assurances that the actions of the Vietnamese government seemed profoundly disturb-ing. He agreed and complained that Hanoi changed its attitude towards religion every day. Indeed, in a further demonstration of Communist hostility, the VCP would not allow him to leave the country to accept a teaching position in the U.S. Despite his life-long commitment to peace, he favored U.S. intervention in 1965 because he believed that the U.S. had defended South Vietnam from a foreign invader: North Vietnam. No doubt, like many contemporary Vietnamese, he found American interference in South Vietnam much more palatable after enduring a quarter century of Communism.

Unlike Thich Quang Lien, many religious people in Vietnam censored themselves rather than risk the ire of the VCP. In 1996, at the Phap Van pagoda in Ho Chi Minh City, an earnest and intelligent young monk, named Thich Nguyen Tang, who spoke excellent English introduced himself to me. Throughout our talk, he steered clear of any kind of political discussion, although he did acknowledge that he wanted to study in Australia. The monk was also in the process of compiling a book about Buddhism around the world and composed articles for a local Buddhist publication as well. When he asked me to contribute an article on Buddhism in America, I readily agreed. As I left, I noticed a photograph of the famous Vietnamese Buddhist philosopher Thich Nhat Hanh hanging on his wall.

That afternoon, the assistant editor of *Giac Ngo*, a Buddhist weekly published in Ho Chi Minh City, interviewed me for his publication. Thich Tam Thien mentioned that he wanted to study in America but, like many of the clerics, carefully avoided any discussion of politics. He argued that, under the VCP, all religions retained the same status. In a weird kind of way, that may have been true, in that every creed received extraordinarily close scrutiny from the security services. Yet to assert that the Vietnamese enjoyed religious freedom seemed ludicrous.

When the Thich Tam Thien and Thich Nguyen Tang later met me, they greeted me in a very solemn manner. In response to their request, I had written an article for their journal about my work on the Buddhist peace movement. Both told me that many of my words could not be published in Vietnam, such as references to Thich Nhat Hanh or Bao Ninh and his searing account of the conflict: *The Sorrow of War*.

This information truly astonished me given that Bao Ninh's book could be purchased on any street corner in Hanoi and that Thich Nhat Hanh's works had been widely published in Vietnam and his picture hung on one of the monk's wall. Nevertheless, they adamantly claimed that publication of my innocuous words would cause misfortune to rain down on them and me. Finally, one of them said, "You want to come back, don't you?" Realizing that the

VCP might reject my subsequent attempts to return to Vietnam and that my article could place the monks in considerable danger, I grudgingly agreed to rewrite the piece and deleted the offending passages.

After my return to the US, I e-mailed Vo Van Ai, a Vietnamese human rights activist and outspoken critic of the VCP who published a Vietnamese language journal in Paris called *Que Me* (Fatherland). He had been closely connected to Buddhist peace activists during the war and had earlier provided me with valuable information for my dissertation. When he heard about my experiences, he suggested an article for his journal. The final product, "Religious Freedom in Vietnam?" ("Tu Do Ton Giao Tai Viet Nam?") severely criticized the VCP for its brutal suppression of the outlawed Unified Buddhist Church (UBC) but also pointed out that many Vietnamese censored themselves to avoid government scrutiny. Vo Van Ai translated my essay into Vietnamese and published it.

Buddhist novices at the Phap Van Pagoda—Ho Chi Minh City, 1996

Briefly before I departed the U.S. on my 1997 trip to Vietnam, Vo Van Ai warned me that the Cong An would likely have a copy of the article by the time I arrived in Vietnam. He cautioned that the police could well pick me up for a heart-to-heart discussion about my critique of the Communist Party. Although convinced that he had exaggerated the reach of the Cong An, as my plane approached Vietnamese airspace, possible repercussions from the essay began to worry me. On the last part of the flight, I awoke from a troubled sleep just as the movie *Space Jam* ended with Ray Kelly's song, "I believe I can fly." Although I was struck by the irony of such a quintessentially American film being broadcast on Vietnam Airlines, suddenly, I realized that my plane had entered Vietnam where my worst nightmares resided. As my apprehension grew, I wondered if Vo Van Ai might be right and that the police could cause me some severe problems in Ho Chi Minh City. I underwent a few hours of acute trepidation before finally passing through Vietnamese immigration. There nothing serious happened, prompting me to forget about it.

Nonetheless, a few weeks after my return to the US, an urgent letter from one of the monks arrived that warned me, "Don't write another word." To my great shock and surprise, the journal con-

Vegetarian breakfast in Ho Chi Minh City—1996

taining my article had been smuggled into Vietnam, and the Cong An had obtained a copy. Afterwards, the police started questioning everyone who knew me to find out more about my activities. At one point, a policeman told my associate, "We know everything about Robert Topmiller," and then went through my essay line by line with the holy man. My salvation derived from the line I utilized to preface all of my interviews, wherein I assured those who spoke with me that I was only interested in history, not politics. Luckily that statement appeared in my article, and the cleric used it to defend his association with me.

Fortunately, this story had a happy ending, as both monks eventually relocated outside of Vietnam. Thich Tam Thien now lives in the U.S., and Thich Nguyen Tang resides in Australia. Unfortunately, the Australian monk later discovered that the VCP had banned him from Vietnam for ten years because of outspoken criticism of the Hanoi regime. For a Vietnamese steeped in the extraordinarily close family web of a Confucian and Ancestor Worshiping society, a forced separation from family for a decade represented a unacceptable and incalculable affront. Incredibly, the Vietnamese government issued him a visa and then told him to get out of the country when he arrived at the airport in Vietnam.

On a later trip to Vietnam, Thich Nguyen Tang related numerous stories about VCP harassment of his pagoda in Ho Chi Minh City. Often, the Cong An raided the temple in the middle of the night and forced the monks to answer numerous roll calls. Even more distressing, when the monk could not find a childhood friend and contacted the Cong An, they assured him that they knew his location exactly, in a chilling demonstration of their ability to monitor individual behavior in a country of over 80 million people.

In 1997, however, I only understood that the police might know about my article. The other details did not become clear until several years later. Needless to say, I remained pretty nervous during my subsequent trips in view of the fact that, as I constantly reminded myself, my number one goal in life was/is avoiding jail in Vietnam, hence my eagerness to quickly resolve any difficulties with the police before they checked too closely into my background.

Thich Quang Do

Of course, my risks seemed insignificant compared to the torment the Communists have inflicted on people of conscience in Vietnam. In January 1992, Thich Quang Do, a prominent UBC leader, published an open letter to Prime Minister Vo Van Kiet of Vietnam that detailed the long history of religious and political repression in Vietnam under the Vietnamese Communist Party. He ended his manifesto with a courageous call for religious freedom in his country. The monk subsequently received a five-year prison term for his actions. During the same period, other members of the UBC came forward with complaints about religious persecution and likewise suffered incarceration.

Approaching Vietnam's most famous dissident proved difficult. During a 1996 chat in Ho Chi Minh City with Professor Minh Chi, a widely acknowledged expert on Vietnamese Buddhism, I had brought up the status of Thich Quang Do and Thich Huyen Quang, the imprisoned leaders of the dissident Vietnamese Buddhists. As soon as the words issued from my mouth, in a state of utter incredulity he blurted out "You know about them?" and then softly, "I know them very well. They are fine scholars and good men."

Abruptly, he stopped and said, "This is very difficult to talk about." Three years later, he claimed that, as a result of our earlier conversation, the police had visited him. But it did not matter, he said, because, "I am an old man and they can't do anything to me."

Minh Chi and author (Ho Chi Minh City, 1996)

Vietnamese authorities released Thich Quang Do from prison in August 1998, as part of a general amnesty of political prisoners to commemorate the regime's anniversary. When I discovered that he had been set free, the likelihood of interviewing him during my next trip to Vietnam in March 1999 seemed possible. To my great surprise, when I landed in Ho Chi Minh City, it seemed even grimmer than it had been during my previous visits. Indeed, the city had suffered a severe financial downturn after the onset of the Asian financial crisis in 1997, when a combination of lost investment, declining exports, greatly decreased tourism, and inept Communist management of the financial system had slowed Vietnam's economy and created vast human suffering. An absolutely stunning number of homeless children inhabited the city in 1999, but by 2002 they had mostly disappeared from the increasingly prosperous and traveler-friendly Ho Chi Minh City. Many Vietnamese suspected that Hanoi shipped them to the countryside or to concentration camps far from the city to spur the growth of tourism.

Interestingly, while walking downtown one evening, I felt uneasy about the possibility of being robbed. People in my hotel had given me dire warnings about "motorcycle hooligans." As my angst grew, I realized—with no small amount of irony—that I had always been afraid in Vietnam, just for different reasons.

After much soul searching, I casually strolled one morning through the front door of the Thanh Minh Zen Monastery in Ho Chi Minh City; a nun escorted me upstairs and offered me a seat. I had been in town for a few days and had debated whether to visit Vietnam's most prominent dissident. The police could have blocked my entry, but I counted on the fact that the security forces represented a huge bureaucracy that might react slowly to my admission to the country. Some people hung around the entrance eyeing me suspiciously, but no one made a move to prevent my walking in.

Soon afterward, Thich Quang Do entered the room, welcomed me with a firm handshake and a cordial greeting, and asked me to join him on the sofa because he suffered from deafness in one ear as a result of a beating he received in prison. I expected that a man who had endured years of imprisonment and isolation would be serious, sober and traumatized. Instead, he projected warmth, friendliness, kindness, and commitment to his principles.

Thanh Minh Zen Monastery (Ho Chi Minh City, 1999)

With little probing, he launched into a spirited denunciation of the Communists. The week before, when he tried to speak to his fellow Buddhist leader Thich Huyen Quang, the police detained him for five days and barred him from contacting his friend. He also described the difficulties the UBC experienced with the Communists after 1975, pointing out that Hanoi oppressed Buddhists almost immediately after taking power, precluding them from carrying out their religious functions, seizing their property and imprisoning their leadership. In time, security forces raided pagodas, closed orphanages, disbanded religious organizations, and placed prominent Buddhist leaders under house arrest or imprisonment in remote locations. After 1975, Thich Quang Do spent extended periods of time in prison. Despite his recent liberation from jail, he had suffered continuous harassment from security forces, who had tapped his phone and constantly monitored his movements.

Thich Quang Do and author (Ho Chi Minh City, 1999)

Worst of all, from the dissident's standpoint, the new regime established a government sponsored and controlled Buddhist church that became the only recognized Buddhist religious association in the country. In fact, the monk could not even estimate how many members still belonged to the UBC because the continuing repression in the country had prevented many supporters from publicly identifying themselves. To him, the creation of the puppet church represented one of the most insidious acts of the party in that monks and nuns who supported the government took over the official functions of the church and its property, while those who remained loyal to the UBC suffered persecution. As he argued, the existence of an official church meant, "Monks oppress other monks." In many ways, he expressed the views of countless Vietnamese who had grown weary of government repression but remained afraid to speak out, attempting to plead their case before a world that had become indifferent to their plight under Communism.

In his most pointed and poignant argument, he declared that 58,000 Americans died to bring freedom to South Vietnam, yet the U.S. later aided the Communists, who used the cash to trample on Vietnamese freedom. He asserted that every dime Americans contributed to Vietnam went into the pockets of party members, while nothing filtered down to the people who suffered government oppression and terrorization. In his eyes, U.S. support for the regime perpetuated its power and increased its ability to crush the people. Thus, he pleaded with me to remind the world of the situation in his tortured land.

His bold talk made me extremely nervous, particularly when he told me that the Cong An would most likely arrest me as soon as I emerged from the monastery. My regard for his incredible courage and steadfastness in the face of fierce persecution grew as we spoke. Yet, he deflected my praise with protests of humility and seemed unfazed by the obvious danger he courted by speaking so freely.

Finally, the time came for me to take my leave from this extraordinary human being. As we walked down the stairs, he clutched my arm and asked me to remember my promise to him. Would I keep it? Would I tell the world about the plight of Buddhism in Vietnam?

What else could I say but yes?

Obviously, not everyone had been intimidated by VCP repression, but I wondered if the world would listen.

My apprehension over the possibility of being detained grew as we reached the ground floor. Perhaps sensing my unease, the monk suggested departing in a taxi. The nun called a cab, and minutes later it roared into the courtyard. Thich Quang Do barked instructions to the driver and then told me to get in quickly. I hunkered down in the back seat as we tore out of the monastery and took a wild ride through the city, flying down back alleys and following a circuitous route back to my hotel. I spent an anxious few days waiting to depart from the country and breathed a huge sigh of relief when my flight finally cleared Vietnamese airspace.

Unfortunately, this story did not have a happy ending.

The same week as my meeting with the cleric, a foreign radio station broadcast an interview he had given to one of its correspondents. Afterwards, the authorities cut off his telephone and surrounded the monastery with twenty-four-hour security. Some of his many admirers outside of Vietnam later nominated Thich Quang Do for the Nobel Peace Prize. Yet as I write this book in 2006, he and all of the top leadership of the UBC remain confined in Vietnam.

Religious Dissidents

Although Buddhists suffered dearly under Communism, the VCP assault on religion touched every spiritual group in Vietnam. Nevertheless, Vietnam continued to be one of the most religiously diverse societies on earth and the home of two important homegrown religious movements: the Cao Dai and Hoa Hao Buddhism.

During one research trip to Vietnam, I visited the Cao Dai Holy See in Tay Ninh, close to the Cambodian border. According to its founder, Ngo Van Chieu, the religion originated in Saigon after he encountered the Great Spirit, Cao Dai, during a séance in 1925. At that time, Cao Dai instructed his followers to set up a new religious establishment. Interestingly, the early supporters saw their religious organization as a Buddhist reform movement, although many of their concepts and forms came from Taoism, Confucianism and Catholicism. Cao Dai followers viewed their religion as the amalgamation of all of the world's creeds and as history's ultimate revelation, which attempted to meld the religions of the East and the West into one coherent belief system. Yet, it also reflected the deep Vietnamese adherence to spiritism and the belief that innumerable supernatural entities inhabited the world.

In time, the Cao Dai created a hierarchy of pope, cardinals, bishops, priests and nuns that showed a remarkable similarity to Roman Catholicism, while also establishing a pantheon of spirits that included such diverse individuals as Victor Hugo, Sun Yat Sen, the Buddha, and Confucius. Toward the end of the 1920s, the Cao Dai moved their headquarters to Tay Ninh and built their great cathedral, which became noted as one of the most spectacular sites in Asia. Tay Ninh sits in the shadow of Nui Ba Den (Black Lady Mountain), an area of profound religious significance for many Vietnamese. Before long, the Cao Dai constructed the Cao Dai Holy See in the midst of an absolutely magnificent religious compound in Tay Ninh.

Making contact with the remnants of the true Cao Dai leadership proved exceedingly difficult. Unfortunately, because of their deep anti-Communist stance during the war, the VCP aimed to destroy the church hierarchy after the conflict. In fact, Hanoi executed several high-ranking members while most of the leadership suffered long prison terms while also creating a puppet church staffed by Communist operatives. Not surprisingly, an underground Cao Dai church emerged to represent the real Cao Dai believers.

In December 2000, armed with the names of a couple of the leaders of the real Cao Dai, I attempted to interview them at their home in Tay Ninh. One had recently been released from jail after serving eighteen years, while the other had spent eleven years incarcerated. They appeared totally traumatized from their prison experiences. The mere act of opening up my notebook absolutely terrified them because of the horrors the Communists had inflicted upon them. Finally, after much prodding, they agreed to discuss the history of the Cao Dai but refused to comment about the situation under the VCP. In the middle of my efforts to pry information out of the two men, my driver walked into the courtyard, and both jumped to their feet convinced that the Cong An had arrived to arrest them. I assured them that he was my driver from Ho Chi Minh City and a former ARVN—sans his trigger finger.

But the moment had passed. They seemed skeptical when I tried to salvage something from the meeting by maintaining that the newly elected Bush administration would likely be more committed to human rights than its predecessor. Given that this conversation took place before 9/11, none of us realized how much the world was going to change in the next year.

The Hoa Hao

I encountered many instances of Communist repression in modern Vietnam but few so poignant as the cases of several Hoa Hao Buddhists I met on a research trip to the Mekong Delta in 2000. As my book on the Buddhist peace movement neared completion, it seemed logical to examine Hoa Hao Buddhism, which had stood as a bastion of anti-communism in South Vietnam because the Communists kidnapped and probably murdered their founder, Thay Huynh Phu So, in 1947.

As early as the later part of the nineteenth century, the unsettled condition of the Mekong Delta under French colonialism produced numerous holy men and prophets offering apocalyptic views of the future. Often, the prophets performed miraculous healings or led movements that manifested popular anger over the extreme poverty and exploitation of the area's peasants. In the nineteenth century, a holy man and mystic called the Buddha Master of Western Peace created the Buu Son Ky Huong cult, which eventually evolved into Hoa Hao Buddhism. A charismatic young healer named Huynh Phu So later claimed to be the reincarnation of the Buddha Master when he emerged from the mountains to lead a powerful religious movement that exploded onto the scene on the eve of WWII.

Founded in 1939, Hoa Hao Buddhism matched the conditions and lifestyle of the peasantry of the area well. Realizing that acute privation and ties to the land prevented many peasants from participating in Buddhist rites, Huynh Phu So called for religious practice bereft of clergy and temples. Instead, he combined ancestor worship with Buddhist ritual and invited his followers to observe their religion at home. Thus, the Hoa Hao had no priests, statues, or temples. At the same time, stories of miraculous healing on the part of Huynh Phu So greatly enhanced his reputation with the people of the region. In addition, the sect did not focus on Buddhist sutras (verses); instead its followers mainly studied the teachings of the founder, whose words had been mostly transmitted in the form of easily understood poems.

The extreme hardship of their lives led many peasants to endorse the cult of Maitreya, which believed that a compassionate Buddha would some day deliver people from their suffering. Thus, they looked to the future because their present lives remained so bleak. This dovetailed nicely into a belief that Thay Huynh Phu So would return someday as a Buddha to lead his followers to a land of peace and prosperity very much like the Western Land subscribed to by Pure Land Buddhists. Indeed, Hoa Hao Buddhism represented an extremely complex amalgamation of earlier Buddhist teachings aimed at delivering believers from lives of bitterness into a better future. In many ways, this belief system constituted an extremely rational and sophisticated solution to the problems of this world and the Mekong Delta in particular.

My December 2000 trip to Vietnam came at the end of a year of extreme tension between the VCP and the Hoa Hao. In 1999, when a group of elders attempted to celebrate the sixtieth anniversary of the founding of their religion, local Communist Party operatives physically abused and imprisoned many Hoa Hao leaders, leading to still larger protests and even more demands for religious freedom from others in the community. Not wanting any free expression of religious ideas, the VCP created an official board made up of its own members to ensure that the sect stayed under its control. Yet they failed, as more Hoa Hao who characterized themselves as the "true Hoa Hao Buddhists" demonstrated against the government, including one woman who attempted suicide, another who immolated herself, and others who tried to contact President Bill Clinton during his trip to Vietnam shortly before he left office.

In Ho Chi Minh City, I interviewed Tran Huu Duyen, a Hoa Hao leader for close to seventy years. He had known the founder of the sect, had commanded a Hoa Hao battalion after WW II, and had fought against Ngo Dinh Diem, who imprisoned him and condemned him to death. Fortunately, for Tran and many Hoa Hao prisoners, Diem was overthrown and murdered by rebellious ARVN in 1963, allowing Tran and other Hoa Hao to return to their homeland and continue the fight against the Communists. Indeed, although Tran had initially joined the faith to fight for "peace, freedom, and independence against the French," he later he broke with the Communists because they tried to create divisions between the Hoa Hao, the Cao Dai, and other groups who opposed French colonialism.

When we approached the end of our meeting, Tran looked over at me and said with deep feeling, "When you get to Hoa Hao land, just remember that there is more than one Hoa Hao church," an allusion to the government-appointed board and the opposition "true Hoa Hao." At that point I laid down my pen and said, "I don't think I'll write that down," and "You know, last year I interviewed Thich Quang Do, and I study the Vien Hoa Dao (VHD, the political arm of the outlawed Unified Buddhist Church)." Despite his almost two decades of reeducation, the mere mention of the VHD inspired him to launch into a scorching denunciation of the Communists, accusing them of attacking religion through

Tran Huu Duyen and author (Ho Chi Minh City, 2000)

imprisonment, intimidation, and the creation of puppet churches that served the needs of the government rather than the people. Warming to his topic, he detailed the long train of VCP abuses heaped on the Hoa Hao after 1975, including his long imprisonment in a concentration camp because of his religious beliefs.

His openness in expressing a desire to practice religion without government interference and his remarkable courage in courting another prison stint by being so outspoken moved me deeply and scared me considerably. Regrettably, he also expressed appreciation for President Clinton's non-existent effort to raise human-rights issues with the Hanoi regime. I could not bring myself to let him know that Clinton had passed on the opportunity to stand up for American values while in Vietnam.

The next day, my guide in the Mekong Delta city of Long Xuyen, close to the Hoa Hao Holy Land, contacted me. He seemed like a good choice because he had once taught English and had worked for the U.S. during the American War. Surprisingly, he refused my request to visit the Hoa Hao Holy Land and insisted we visit Chau Doc along the Cambodian border and Sam Mountain instead. I began to wonder about his stability as we made the long drive to Chau Doc; he spoke initially in English, then suddenly switched in mid-sentence to Vietnamese. Of even greater concern, as we toured temples in the Chau Doc area, he prevented people from speaking to me. On other occasions, he interrupted my conversations with people. Even worse, when translating for me, he did not ask questions I posed and gave me abrupt translations of long responses from people.

To my utter astonishment, I soon learned that his peculiarity stemmed from psychological torture inflicted on him by the VCP. When the Communists seized the region in 1975, they devised particularly devilish forms of torture to punish the prophet's family. In my guide's case, given that he had been related to the founder, Hanoi forced him to account for years of activities in a written statement. When he completed his tome, they instructed him to start over again and then compared his first confession with the second declaration to look for inconsistencies, which they attacked with vigor. Eventually, he became unhinged in the process.

All of this occurred because he was related to the founder of Hoa Hao Buddhism, who had not been seen since 1947. After I returned to Ho Chi Minh City, I visited Tran Huu Duyen again with a much greater appreciation for his efforts to protect his religion. We had another fruitful discussion, this time assisted by his son Tai. When I asked Tran about the founder, he pointed out that many Hoa Hao believed that Thay Huynh Phu So still lived and would come back someday. Others considered him a Buddha. Tran argued that the prophet had the ability to change his appearance "like a god," thus it remained hard to pinpoint his character because of his magical nature.

At the end of our meeting, Tai asked me to attend a small service commemorating the birth of the founder that night. But when we later met, Tai informed me that the local Hoa Hao leader had refused to allow me to attend out of fear that the Cong An would observe me entering the house and raid the meeting. Thus, fear of VCP repression had again convinced some people to censor themselves, an effective indication of the power and reach of the Cong An.

Even though we missed the service, Tai graciously took me to dinner, and the next day, I hired him to be my cyclo/driver-translator for the day. Tai, in many ways, exemplified postwar Vietnam. An extremely thoughtful, articulate man who spoke three languages, he worked as a cyclo driver because of his former service in the South Vietnamese Navy. That night, as we ate dinner in an especially poverty-stricken section of Saigon, a group of children and old ladies approached our table and held out their hands. Although we both said no, they just stood there. Finally, when we finished our meal and got ready to leave, Tai nodded at them and they rushed the table to devour our leftover food. One of my most indelible images of Vietnam came from the aftermath of that dinner, when I observed an impossibly old woman chugging the rest of my beer.

That night, as I left Vietnam, I felt relieved to clear Vietnamese airspace once again with my notes and pictures intact; no longer having to worry about the Cong An. In many ways, my trip showed the two paths open to Vietnamese: resistance to the VCP that will eventually bring freedom, or acquiescence which might prolong their brutal tyranny. Nevertheless, members of the "true Hoa Hao Church" had fearlessly defied the VCP to keep the memory of Thay Huynh Phu So alive while awaiting his return.

These experiences told the story of the war's losers. I also wondered how the winners fared. Had the conflict really been decided because a strong, united and forceful North Vietnam defeated a weak corrupt South Vietnam? What did it take for the North Vietnamese to defeat the US, I asked myself? Few of us had enough personal knowledge of the PAVN or Vietnamese history in 1968 to realize that many of the soldiers who came south to fight us at Khe Sanh traveled down the Ho Chi Minh Trail, a pathway maintained mostly by young women.

CHAPTER 8

The Peoples Army of Vietnam

"We belonged to the Ho Chi Minh Brigade."
- Female PAVN veteran, 2005

Many commentators have noted the enhanced status of women throughout Vietnam's history that particularly emerged during times of war and foreign invasion. One Vietnamese proverb, "When war strikes close to home, even the women must fight," illustrated the need for every Vietnamese to support efforts to resist external threats. During the struggle with the US, numerous women continued this tradition by joining the National Liberation Front (the NLF, better known as the Viet Cong) and the PAVN. Some historians estimate that women constituted as much as 50 percent of the NLF. In fact, the Women's Museum in Ho Chi Minh City (HCMC), Vietnam, featured numerous photos and exhibits of women fighting the Americans. Three floors of displays powerfully conveyed the image of the heroic female who upheld home and country.

North Vietnamese women fought in large numbers during the American conflict. In her landmark work on their contributions to the fight against the US, historian Karen Gottschang Turner estimated that over 1.5 million women worked in various combat roles throughout the hostilities and confirmed the vital wartime tasks carried out by women that enabled North Vietnam to craft its astonishing victory over the Americans. Because of the severe manpower needs caused by the American onslaught against North Vietnam, Ho Chi Minh, early in the war, appealed for volunteers to save the nation. According to Turner, thousands of young women answered the call and served in a multitude of jobs, particularly as anti-aircraft gunners, medical personnel, and guides and engineers along the Ho Chi Minh Trail.

In the process, Turner detailed the amazing heroism and sacrifices of women who suffered heavy casualties as they braved years of ferocious American bombing to perform their duties.

Heroic Vietnamese mother (Ho Chi Minh City, 2002)

Tragically, the effects of living and fighting in the jungle for close to a decade caused female veterans to suffer deeply after the hostilities. Many found themselves unable to marry and have children in a society that scorned and pitied childless and unmarried women. Others chose not to have children out of fear of the lingering effects of defoliants and the high incidence of birth defects suffered by those who served in areas where the Americans had sprayed Agent Orange. Many women descended into poverty after 1975 as the success of the revolution cost them the gains they had realized during the fighting. No longer needed to support the conflict, they sank to the bottom of the economic ladder in a desperately poor Vietnam. Some also shared the enormous disillusionment that seized many Vietnamese as they reflected on the price of victory over the Americans. Moreover, Turner asserted that the Vietnamese government denied North Vietnamese women both compensation and recognition for their wartime help.

In 2005, I visited Ho Chi Minh's birthplace outside of Vinh. The city had operated as a critical port in the old North Vietnam and the staging point for supplies heading down the Ho Chi Minh Trail. Given that Vinh had been almost completely leveled by U.S. air and naval attacks during the war, I did not expect a warm welcome. Yet, when I arrived at Ho's home village, I came across a large group of PAVN veterans, including a number of women who proudly displayed their medals on their jackets and blouses. When I told them that I had been in the American military, several of the women proudly exclaimed, "We belonged to the Ho Chi Minh

Brigade," which had been charged with defending the Ho Chi Minh Trail.

None of the women demonstrated any hostility towards me, although a few of the men were clearly upset that they had shaken hands with me after they discovered my nationality. However, my guide had gone through the local vendor stalls informing everyone that I was a professor studying the history of Vietnam. Given that Vietnam developed within the overarching halo of Confucianism, everyone afforded me great respect as a scholar and teacher.

On the drive back to Hue down the old Ho Chi Minh Trail, which had been converted into a super highway, my driver stopped at a friend's café and introduced me to the owner. After

PAVN vets (Vinh, 2005)

Ho Chi Minh Highway (2005)

we had drunk a warm beer and I had told the proprietor about all of my illegal research, I realized that he was an undercover cop. My confidence that the policeman would not likely mess up his friend's profitable venture of driving me all over central Vietnam tempered my trepidation on the way back to Hue. Nevertheless, I remained certain that the police officer received part of my fare.

PAVN heroes (Vinh, 2005)

Encounters with PAVN

My first introduction to North Vietnamese of either gender occurred at Khe Sanh in 1968, when I noticed two enemy soldiers tied up and guarded by Marine MP's outside of the command bunker. Interestingly, the sentries had been assigned to keep watch over our opponents, not preventing them from escaping, but keeping the Marines from killing our recent tormentors. At the time, the rumor mill argued that they had not reached puberty; in fact, they appeared to be adolescents, perhaps fifteen or sixteen years old and rather innocent and frail. It seemed hard to believe that these fragile, sickly teenagers had caused us so much grief. However, years later a former North Vietnamese medic in Hanoi claimed that he had only been a sixteen-year-old when he came south to fight against us at Khe Sanh.

In the intervening years, I stumbled across the radioactively antiwar novel, *The Sorrow of War,* by a former North Vietnamese soldier named Bao Ninh. His grippingly chaotic story began with a group of PAVN vets looking for the corpses of their MIA friends. As the story progressed, it became obvious that the protagonist Kien remained deeply troubled by the war and suffered from PTSD. Indeed, this stunningly antiheroic account of combat exposed the fatalism and guilt felt by so many veterans, but also examined the heartbreak of PTSD: flashbacks, emotional detachment, the inability to form lasting relationships, nightmares, substance abuse, a propensity to violence, and extreme alienation. It was astonishing for many readers of the book to realize that the victors had suffered as deeply as the losers. In the end, Kien only retained a feeling of immense loss of his friends, his youth and, most of all, his innocence. Indeed, the war represented the great divide in his life. Throughout he desperately wanted to return to his prewar sanity, but even that small victory eluded him.

Many students find this messy book, which paralleled the lives of so many American veterans, a difficult read. I assigned it to all of the students in my Vietnam War course. Many hated the book until they completed it, and then some loved it. But few could fathom the disorderly and confused mind of the combat vet who attempted to balance his/her service with the cruel realities of war. Just as Kien wandered through Hanoi in a drunken stupor, many of us lurched through the last four decades trying to find meaning in the senselessness of the Vietnam War and Khe Sanh in particular. I could never accept the price we paid to defend a symbol of American resolve that faded before the year was half over.

Many people think that American veterans developed PTSD because we lost the war. But experiencing Bao Ninh's torment showed the commonality of war's impact on the human psyche. Even though the North Vietnamese won, they still suffered deeply because of the war.

Interestingly, Bao Ninh penned his work during a brief period of intellectual flowering under Doi Moi ("the new thinking," a move from a Marxist-Leninist economic model to one that eventually embraced capitalism). However, the VCP quickly suppressed the movement when the party realized that some authors wanted to use their transitory moment of liberation to question the high cost of victory over the Americans. Indeed, during the war, many Vietnamese believed that if they could defeat the Americans, they could accomplish anything, only later to face the unpleasant reality of postwar Vietnam and the country's precipitous slide into poverty and hunger.

PAVN

My next encounter with Vietnamese soldiers occurred in 1996 when, of course, they no longer belonged to the North Vietnamese Army. After 1975, all soldiers served in the same force: the Peoples Army of Vietnam. Nevertheless, I usually gave them wide berth because of what I perceived to be their antiforeigner disposition and indoctrination and my inclination to believe that many of them still held strong feelings about the American War which had killed so many of their people. Although some Vietnamese still felt profound revulsion towards Americans, their government had instructed its citizens to tone down criticism of the U.S. because it wanted to improve relations with the American government and keep venture capital flowing into the country.

Two impulses influenced my interactions with the Vietnamese in postwar Vietnam. On the one hand, many southerners whose families fought on the side of South Vietnam liked and respected Americans. But some southerners who supported the other side still loathed Americans and particularly begrudged the fact that when Americans came to Vietnam and spent money, they had to wait on them and treat them with courtesy. In fact, some Vietnamese viewed American tourists as the same foreign invaders that devastated their country in the 1960s and 1970s. A number of Vietnamese, in their more honest moments, admitted to me that they disliked bowing and scraping to collect needed dollars from foreigners. It remained no small irony that a revolution that relied on Vietnam's long history of resistance to outsiders for survival now depended on foreign investment and visitors to retain power.

In 2002, as I sat in a restaurant in Hue examining my Khe Sanh pictures taken that day, a young waiter came by and asked to look at my photos, a very common occurrence in Vietnam where little concept of privacy exists. Often wait staff went through my photos and books or looked over my shoulder as I wrote in my journal. But in this instance, when my server discovered that I had been at Khe Sanh and saw pictures of unexploded ordnance at the old base, he became exceedingly emotional because five members of his family had been killed in an American bombing during the hostilities. Certainly, his family had not recovered from the fighting. Nor had they forgiven the U.S.

Not surprisingly, our elusive and mostly unseen adversary from 1968 maintained a high level of visibility in the former South Vietnam. During my visit to Khe Sanh in 1996, when I noticed a Vietnamese soldier walking through Khe Sanh village packing an AK-47, a chill went up my spine that made me wonder why the army had to have such a heavy presence within its own country. But later I came to understand that the Communists feared the mountain people so much that they always wanted to intimidate them and make them feel that they could never move beyond the reach or retribution of the Vietnamese government.

The heavy military presence seemingly appeared everywhere in the south. In 1997, during a jog in a Ho Chi Minh City park, I came upon a platoon of PAVN dry-firing their weapons. It made me so angry that I kept running past them, which impelled them to glare at me with utter hatred. Why did the Vietnamese army have to display its weapons in a park in the middle of the city, I wondered? In fact, in downtown Ho Chi Minh City sat an enormous army base, which existed no doubt to maintain order and prevent any potential internal uprising.

In 2000, on the highway to Tay Ninh, close to the Cambodia border, I spotted a large group of Vietnamese soldiers walking in a sloppy, unmilitary-like formation down the road in the fading sunlight. They did not appear very tough or disciplined. Most likely returning from a day in the field, they allowed their helmets to hang loosely on their backs; some carried their weapons over their shoulders, others under their arms. It seemed hard to believe that this seemingly slapdash, disorganized force had defeated the United States at the height of our military power.

That same year, on the Vietnamese/Cambodian border close to Chau Doc, I climbed Sam Mountain so that I could look down into Cambodia from the crest of the peak. The Vietnamese and Cambodians fought a brutal war in the late 1970s, and Vietnam occupied Cambodia for close to a decade after driving Pol Pot and the Khmer Rouge from power. Thus, the mountain held great strategic value for both sides in any future military confrontation and sat in a very sensitive border area. When I hiked to the top, I noticed that a PAVN army post rested on top of the mountain. The local Vietnamese soldier on duty was sleeping soundly in a hammock in the middle of the day, and nobody appeared to be guarding the border. I took a photo of him, an illegal act in Vietnam where the government prohibited pictures of military installations.

PAVN and concrete trench on the Vietnamese/Cambodian border (2000)

Of course, Vietnam seldom revealed itself at first blush. The hilltop position had a concrete fighting trench at the crest of the ridge, which made me speculate how great it would have been at Khe Sanh if we had possessed solid dugouts rather than our dirt trenches that often collapsed from incoming rounds and buried men alive. I felt forced to ask: How could we have been so poorly prepared to fight at Khe Sanh, when even the Vietnamese army built better fortifications than we had? As I walked around, I noticed air vents and antennas protruding from the ground at different points on the mountain. On the side of the hill, steel doors had been carved into the mountainside. It appeared that the PAVN had tunneled out the inside of the mountain and had established a communications and a supply center inside in case of another conflict with Cambodia.

A year later, while conducting research on the mountain people, I had a much closer experience with the PAVN in Buon Ma Thuot. Because of its position in the Central Highlands, the Vietnamese army considered Buon Ma Thuot a critically strategic location. Indeed, I observed at least eight army bases around the city. I had commenced my research on the Mountain people in Dalat a week earlier, but local VCP operatives forced me to purchase a permit to visit the Montagnard villages around the city. Hence, no one would open up and talk to me, because the local authority had provided me with a party member as a guide.

In my frustration, I decided to remove myself to another location and avoid further contacts with the VCP. I returned to Ho Chi Minh City and flew directly to Buon Ma Thuot, where I hired a driver named Tien. We spent an intriguing week driving around the Central Highlands on the back of his motorcycle, which allowed me to visit a number of minority villages where few Westerners had been in years. In many ways, Tien typified life in postwar Vietnam for southerners. His father had served in the ARVN and had gone to reeducation, so when he reached adulthood, Tien joined the Vietnamese Army to avoid being considered disloyal like his father.

Hence, he fought in Cambodia for four years during the Vietnamese occupation (1978-89) of that country. One afternoon, he commented offhandedly that a lot of Vietnamese died in Cambodia, many more than anybody ever realized. Indeed, the brutal and bloody war that rescued the Cambodian people from the monstrous Khmer Rouge regime of Pol Pot also delayed Vietnam's recovery from the American War and brought it to clash with China. Ironically, during the American War, many Vietnamese believed that their country had been caught in a proxy war between the U.S. and Communist China. Yet, in Cambodia, the U.S. and China joined forces to support the Khmer Rouge against the Vietnamese, plunging Vietnam into another surrogate conflict, this time between the US/China and the Soviet Union.

As I had driven into Buon Ma Thuot on my first day in the city, I noticed a large number of military displays in a park on the outskirts of town. My driver later explained that the PAVN would be celebrating its founding on the following Saturday so the army had sponsored a carnival to put its best foot forward with the local people. Eventually, my driver invited me to attend the commemoration the following weekend.

Considering all that had occurred in 1968 and my continuing dread of the security services, I crossed a momentous psychological barrier by sitting down with members of the PAVN. But, in the end, in what had to be one of my nuttiest acts in Vietnam, I attended the PAVN commemoration and drank beer with a group of Vietnamese soldiers, including three officers. The beer tasted especially good given my nervousness. Yet, I quickly learned that many PAVN, including northerners, sought the reconciliation that I preached about in the U.S. but had found so hard to attain in Vietnam. That afternoon continued the process of stripping away my prejudices towards the Vietnamese.

As it turned out, the young soldiers at the event adopted an extremely friendly stance towards me and wanted to know all about my family, the US, and me. They seemed like wonderful young people and appreciated the fact that an American had come to their party. Eventually one of the soldiers asked me, "You speak Vietnamese so well, why can't you understand it?" I replied, "Oh, I was injured during the war and my eardrums were damaged, so I don't hear very well." When he inquired, "Well, who hurt you?" I responded, "You guys."

They all started laughing nervously because nobody wanted to say anything. To get past our moment of acute embarrassment, they told me what a powerful army the United States had and what great technological power we possessed. For my part, I assured them that the Vietnamese army had great fighting spirit and excellent soldiers, which made them beam with pride. Because they had invited me to be their guest, they broke out the beer, which made me really happy. Unfortunately, they lacked cold beer—that was not the first time someone had offered me warm beer in Vietnam—so they placed a block of ice in a metal tin and then poured the beer over the ice to chill it. Unfortunately, we consumed it so fast that it had little chance to cool. Each person took his/her cup, filled it from the tub, and gave a toast, and then everyone chugged their beer.

I only knew one toast, "Vietnam Muon Nam!" (Vietnam for a thousand years!). Every time I yelled it, they all cheered, gulped down their beer, and looked at me. One person asked, "Why aren't you chugging your beer?" I responded, "I'm too old to chug beer," and like soldiers everywhere, they looked at me with utter astonishment. When I began to say no to their repeated suggestions that I consume more alcohol and protested that I had to catch a plane later in the day, my driver leaned over and whispered "khong cam on" (no thank you) in my ear, reminding me once again that proper etiquette remained critically important to Vietnamese.

Eventually, a young sub Lieutenant sat down next to me, and we conversed in English, discussing Vietnam, the war, and our joy that Americans and Vietnamese could finally become friends. When I prepared to leave, I casually inquired, "What's your job?" He responded with absolutely no emotion, "We're commandos." Anyone who spent time at Khe Sanh can appreciate the role of Vietnamese commandos in any military operation. Almost assuredly, they would be the first people to die in battle.

PAVN (Buon Ma Thuot, 2001)

I found their youth, enthusiasm, and honesty totally disarming perhaps because they resembled so many of us in our prewar innocence. By this point, juxtaposing the contrasts in postwar Vietnam seemed especially difficult given that I had witnessed two extremes: unsurprising ARVN angst and unforeseen PAVN docility. The PAVN did not seem hostile to anyone; they even told me they liked me very much.

A picture of us drinking beer sits on my desk to remind me everyday of one delightful afternoon when I transcended the gap between myself and the PAVN and understood once again that the time had arrived for all of us to move past war and work to achieve reconciliation.

PAVN Vets

I had experienced two earlier and much more emotional encounters with North Vietnamese veterans. As I waited in line at the Vietnam Airlines desk in Seoul, South Korea in 1999, a distinguished-looking Vietnamese man walked up to check in for his flight. As we engaged in a conversation about Vietnam, the US, and President Clinton's planned visit to Vietnam, his expensive suit, rings on several fingers, well-appointed haircut, and overall bearing convinced me that he held an important position in Vietnamese society.

In time, he mentioned that he had served as a PAVN interpreter and had questioned downed American pilots during the war, a statement that bothered me greatly. He quickly pointed out that he saw the war mainly as a mistake between the two governments, not as an issue between the Vietnamese and American people. He also declared that he owned two factories in Vietnam, including one in Ho Chi Minh City. Despite the friendly nature of our encounter, his obvious wealth and good fortune in a Vietnam that remained desperately poor seemed startling. When I mentioned that Doi Moi seemed to have been good for him, he quickly retorted—somewhat like Dick Cheney and just as disingenuously— that he had earned it all on his own and that the government had nothing to do with it.

Our conversation stood in stark contrast to an earlier talk with another PAVN vet. In 1995, I studied Vietnamese in a summer language program at the University of Wisconsin—Madison as one of the requirements for my Ph.D. One of the Vietnamese instructors, Dr. Dinh Van Duc, normally taught at the University of Hanoi and had earned his doctorate in linguistics at the University of Moscow. Naturally, I wondered how a professor from the other side would react to an American veteran. Before long, we had a discussion about the war, and, to my utter amazement, Thay (teacher) Duc told me that his brother had served as a medic with the PAVN during the 1968 siege of Khe Sanh. Thay Duc, who always referred to Khe Sanh as very terrible, told me that his brother, like me, had problems with his hearing ever since. He urged me to contact his brother on my next trip to Vietnam.

Thus, I found myself in 1997 sitting in a hotel lobby in Hanoi waiting to become acquainted with my former adversary. At the appointed hour, a diminutive, well-dressed Vietnamese walked into my hotel and introduced himself as Dr. Dinh Van Toan. A very kind, soft-spoken man, he seemed genuinely delighted to meet me. He explained that he went to Khe Sanh at the end of 1967 with the PAVN and stayed there for a year. Sixteen years old when he joined the army and eighteen when he got out, Toan asserted that Khe Sanh had been a dreadful ordeal for the men in his unit, especially when the B-52's struck. After one more year in the south, he returned to North Vietnam for demobilization and later earned a Ph.D. in geology at the University of Moscow. In 1997, he worked as head of the Geophysical Department at the Institute of Geological Sciences in Hanoi.

Like myself he had not completely recovered from the war. He had me feel pieces of metal still in his back and claimed that he could not hear anything for a year after his return to the north; only gradually had he regained partial hearing. Often hungry at Khe Sanh, Toan and his comrades frequently consumed captured American provisions that had missed the drop point (the landing zone for our supplies). He declared that the rations tasted good, a potent indicator of the quality of meals the North Vietnamese had "enjoyed" during most of the siege. When I advised him about us casualty figures at Khe Sanh, he said that PAVN sustained far greater losses than ours, a statement that did not surprise me, although I avoided pressing him for numbers because I thought that it would be in bad taste.

After I described my Khe Sanh vets group, Toan responded that PAVN vets had an overall organization, but not for Khe Sanh (which he referred to as Tacon, the North Vietnamese word for the base) alone. In an interesting aside he asserted that they had never asked for anything from the government because the veterans "knew that the government could not turn us down," which seemed like a round-about way of rationalizing the inability of Hanoi to provide relief for its veterans. We concluded that a joint reunion where vets from both sides could come together and reminisce on our shared experience would be a good idea, leaving behind much of the hostility between us.

During dinner, Toan asked my opinion of his people, a question posed to me constantly by the Vietnamese. It seemed many Vietnamese worried that we would not like them for defeating us in the war. After I assured him that Vietnamese in the U.S. and Vietnam had treated me with great courtesy and kindness, we both agreed that it was good that our peoples no longer were enemies. Toan observed that most of us survived mainly due to good fortune and that the bitterness between American and Vietnamese veterans should go away, given that politicians on both sides had used us as pawns in a larger game over which we had little control. When I told Toan and Thay Duc about my work on the Buddhist peace movement, they became excited and interested, agreeing on the importance of showing how the conflict could have been prevented so future generations might escape the scourge of war.

Finally, as we discussed our families and our dreams for their future, we began to appreciate that the things that united us seemed far more important than those that separated us. As we left the restaurant, Toan turned and hugged me in a gesture of kindness, shared pain, and understanding. Despite the joy of our meeting, I realized that the conflict for Toan and thousands of Vietnamese and Americans remained a deeply painful memory.

For many years, I wanted to atone to the Vietnamese people for the horrors my country visited upon them. My dinner with Toan epitomized another step in that process. When I first wrote about my meeting with Toan, I titled the piece "Friends and Enemies," to describe my changed feelings towards the Vietnamese, but in truth, I became increasingly unsure which was which. Yet, despite my growing belief in the importance of reconciliation, I knew that the VCP had no intention of forgiving its former adversaries and that some Vietnamese will never find closure from the war.

CHAPTER 9

Remnants

"Something went wrong with the soldiers' minds that day."
- Vietnamese schoolteacher, 2003

Grippingly, government harassment of those who supported the U.S. remained constant, with really not much difference occurring in recent years despite the incredible economic growth Vietnam enjoyed under Market-Leninism. The condition of the mountain people (Americans commonly call them Montagnards, a term the minority people consider pejorative because the French assigned it to them) epitomized one of the more troubling aspects of our involvement in Vietnam. The VCP, an organization that gained considerable support and legitimacy in South Vietnam during the war because of its egalitarian land policies, forgot its promises of a postwar autonomous ethnic region, forcing the mountain people to live in established villages and encouraging ethnic Vietnamese to migrate to traditional Highland areas.

Increasingly, the population of the Central Highlands became an explosive mixture of northern, central, and southern Vietnamese as part of Hanoi's New Economic Program (NEP). Many Highlanders claimed, moreover, that the VCP granted them extremely poor land, while the government's insistence that they settle in permanent villages rather than continue their old practice of moving to more fertile areas over time merely represented a different form of imprisonment exacerbated by the widespread Highlander belief that Vietnamese received favored treatment from the Communists.

However, the land issue revealed a much more complex situation than simple retribution against the Highlanders. In recent years, the VCP eradicated starvation in Vietnam, a remarkable accomplishment considering the population explosion that followed the war. Nevertheless, Hanoi demonstrated extraordinary sensitivity to the political dangers of widespread hunger and thus refused to allow free-market forces to affect rice cultivation in the country. In fact, the government retained control over the whole country's rice crop and only sold the surplus on the world market after ensuring that domestic demand had been met. Consequently, placing more reliable Vietnamese on Highland land made sense to VCP officials, who feared the instability that food shortages could bring and doubted the loyalty of the Highlanders anyway.

Highland woman, south of Khe Sanh (2003)

Yet, coerced absorption, resulting from the VCP's educational and conscription polices, posed a far greater danger for the mountain people than Vietnamese migration into their region. Hanoi required most young men, including ethnic minorities, to complete mandatory military service, which forced indigenous people to assimilate into the dominant culture. At the same time, the VCP compelled many Highland children to attend public schools, where they studied Vietnamese language and culture. As many young people learned to speak Vietnamese, the Highlanders feared that their native languages could be lost in the process. Consequently, their parents witnessed their children moving toward assimilation every time they donned their school uniforms and headed for the local schoolhouse. As a result, many Highlanders held their children out of school to work in the fields and resist Vietnamese absorption.

Many members of the mountain clans feared that their tribes could someday disappear under the VCP policy of forced assimilation, particularly because persistent Communist repression and control of information left outsiders with little knowledge of the Highland peoples' plight. Although Western human-rights groups had scored Hanoi for its suppression of political and religious freedom after 1975, not surprisingly, Hanoi considered Western preaching about human rights as a new form of American imperialism and as interference in its domestic affairs. The government

Highland girl in a Vietnamese school uniform on her way to class (Central Highlands, 2001)

responded to international criticism by projecting the official line that all groups in the country enjoyed equal rights, while touting the fact that the most recent VCP general secretary, Nong Duc Manh, belonged to an ethnic minority group.

Numerous rumors arose that Manh was the illegitimate son of Ho Chi Minh. Supposedly, Ho had a relationship with a Highland woman while living in the mountains of northern Vietnam during WWII. If true, it would mean that two of the few remaining Communist countries, North Korea and Vietnam, adopted hereditary succession to choose their leaders in an extreme example of what historian Douglas Pike termed Confucian Marxism.

The American War

The mountain people split over taking sides in the war with the Americans. Some supported the insurgency, while others cast their lot with the dominant power in the region, hoping to use American power to gain leverage with the South Vietnamese. Thus, many ethnic tribes forged strong bonds with American Special Forces units who lived and worked alongside the mountain people and developed good working relationships with them, while providing them with training and weapons. Washington also assured them that their powerful ally would never abandon them, a promise that the Highlanders recalled with bitterness after 1975.

Regrettably for the mountain people, the Ho Chi Minh Trail traversed much of their territory. Thus, they endured intense American bombardment, which led to extremely high casualties and population displacement along with the heavy losses they encountered in fighting the insurgency. Nor did they retain an especially amicable relationship with the South Vietnamese government; the Highlanders rose up in revolt on a number of occasions during the war. Nevertheless, some 45,000 indigenous troops fought alongside the US, and about 250,000 Highlanders overall died in the conflict.

With the Communist victory in 1975, the situation looked bleak for the mountain people, especially after the American government abandoned their cause.

Moreover, their new Communist overlords viewed them with great suspicion for having supported the Americans. At the same time, like the former ARVN, numerous Highlanders served long terms in foul reeducation camps intended to reform their thinking. After Washington implemented the Orderly Departure Program (ODP) in the late 1980s, mountain people with over two years of reeducation could ostensibly immigrate to the U.S. However, because of the high cost of resettlement, VCP harassment, and the many years that had passed, few ethnic people took advantage of the offer. American immigration policy shifted in the 1990s and became much more restrictive toward Southeast Asia, effectively slowing Highlander movement to the U.S. The U.S. quit taking ODP applications in 1994, despite the fact that thousands of Highlanders still wanted to escape Communist tyranny by migrating to the U.S.

Interestingly, some of the mountain people carried out armed resistance against the Vietnamese after 1975. As the Communists consolidated control of postwar Vietnam, the Highlanders continued fighting until Vietnamese military pressure and heavy casualties forced them to retreat into Cambodia. After war broke out between Cambodia and Vietnam in 1978, their cause gained new life when the Khmer Rouge provided them with limited sanctuary, along with some military support. Astonishingly, elements of the mountain people waged sporadic guerilla warfare against Vietnamese forces until the early 1990s.

Bru children outside of Khe Sanh (2002)

When United Nations (UN) personnel entered Cambodia in the early part of the decade to establish a stable government, they discovered, to the shock of many international observers, that a Cambodian enclave still existed from which the Highlanders launched periodic raids on Vietnam. In 1991, when the last Highland rebels surrendered to UN authorities, only about four hundred fighters remained of the original ten thousand who opted out of cooperating with the Communists in 1975.

On our last day together, Tien took me to a Highland village inhabited by members of the Ede tribe. As I walked down a path by the settlement, a striking-looking Highlander who had worked for the U.S. during the war greeted me in perfect English. At first, he seemed reluctant to talk about the situation after 1975, but after I sent Tien to town to buy some cigarettes, our former ally commented sardonically that my money could be better spent on medicine than cigarettes. But I mainly wanted Tien out of the way so that the Highlander would feel free to talk.

According to him, the village had supported the U.S. and many Americans lived and worked there before 1975. After serving the U.S. for ten years, he spent another six in reeducation. He claimed that he wanted to immigrate to the U.S. but could not because his large family of five daughters put tremendous pressure on him to generate wealth, while his status as a non-person rendered him almost helpless to support his family.

During our discussion, his desperation and angst seemed almost palpable. Even though the area around the village had always been Ede land, he asserted that the tribe had lost control of its ancestral territory when Hanoi allotted a mere three acres for each family to farm. Even worse, "no tigers, snakes, or jungle [existed] anymore," and few elephants remained to hunt, denying the Highlanders of important food sources while also preventing them from engaging in their ancient tradition of pursuing wild game. The Ede particularly resented the migration of northern Vietnamese into the area. As a result, "everyday Ede people fle[d] into Cambodia," reflecting the constant tensions between the new immigrants and the mountain people.

Heavy VCP pressure on the mountain people had led to an explosion of protest just months earlier. In February 2001, thou-

Highlander (Central Highlands, 2001)

Ede family (Central Highlands, 2001)

sands of enraged Highlanders lashed out against ongoing oppression as decades of frustration ignited massive demonstrations in the Central Highlands. The VCP responded with increased repression, arbitrary arrests, torture, and long prison terms for many of the protesters. As a result, hundreds of mountain people again fled into Cambodia, where human-rights organizations established camps to absorb the influx of refugees. Although Cambodia initially cooperated with the UN and human rights groups to assist the migrants, eventually Hanoi persuaded Phnom Penh to close the camps and block further escapes from Vietnam. At the same time, Vietnamese forces slipped into Cambodia to kidnap and return Highlanders to Vietnam, while Hanoi insisted that no mountain people had fled the country.

Religious Repression

Numerous mountain people had embraced Christianity in the twentieth century, a situation that caused them great difficulties after 1975. Many found the liberating doctrines of Christianity attractive while receiving significant support from Highlanders outside of Vietnam who smuggled Bibles and other religious tracts into the country. According to the U.S. State Department, Protestants constituted only 1 percent of Vietnam's population, but ethnic minorities comprised two-thirds of Vietnamese Protestants, including 200,000 adherents in the Central Highlands.

One of the most dramatic developments in recent years had been the explosive growth of Evangelical Protestantism among the minority people. To the VCP, this represented an alarming and dangerous development because, like the mountain people, the Communists mainly associated Protestantism with Americans. Moreover, the party continued to be particularly sensitive about any form of religious activity or manifestations of religious pluralism, fearing that any religious movement had the potential to unleash the underlying tensions in Vietnamese society, which might lead to widespread instability and the collapse of the regime. Indeed, Hanoi had embarked on a vigorous persecution of religion shortly after taking over South Vietnam in 1975, so that the mountain people suffered oppression both for their war service and religious beliefs.

As a result of harsh repression, including beatings and arbitrary arrests of Protestants by local authorities, minority people initiated a home church movement: they worshiped privately and avoided the pervasive presence of the security forces, which closely monitored every religious structure in Vietnam. Nevertheless, the VCP attempted to curb religious activity among the Highlanders by tearing down their churches and homes and compelling some Highlanders to forsake their beliefs. Many churches were padlocked during the day to avoid unauthorized usage, while other church buildings appeared totally forlorn and abandoned. To ensure compliance with government restrictions on religious activities, Highland areas exhibited extremely heavy concentrations of regular army troops and the security police.

Empty Highlander church in the Central Highlands (2001)

Ironically, as I wrote this chapter in 2004, the BBC World News reported another deadly confrontation in the Central Highlands between the Highlanders and the VCP.

The Communists would have appeared less than human if they had not harbored suspicions about the loyalty of the mountain people. Yet, their tyrannical methods brought about more rebellion and oppression. Indeed, the mountain people faced an uncertain and dangerous future and also the potential that their unique way of life could disappear under Communism in Vietnam. Like so many of the war's participants, they continued to suffer from its impact long after the departure of their American allies.

Cong Giao

Of all of the groups that have suffered under the VCP, Vietnamese Catholics may be the most demoralized. In March 1997, I visited Phu Cam village, a Catholic enclave in Hue centered on the enormous Phu Cam Cathedral, founded in 1624. The religious structure featured a monument to all of the former bishops of Hue, including Ngo Dinh Thuc, Ngo Dinh Diem's brother and the man who sparked the Buddhist Crisis of 1963 that eventually led to an expanded U.S. intervention in South Vietnam.

Not surprisingly, the VCP severely oppressed Catholics after 1975 while loyalty and affection for the U.S. remained particularly high among the small Roman Catholic population of Hue. In fact, two Roman Catholic prelates in the city claimed that they had concealed American soldiers in their religious compounds as the PAVN overwhelmed the city in 1968.

One of the individuals, a Roman Catholic priest, represented one of the most colorful and daring people I encountered in post-war Vietnam. After our initial meeting in 1997, we remained in close contact through his efforts to help his fellow Vietnamese. He maintained a huge social welfare network in central Vietnam, attempting to connect his parishioners with people outside the country. At one point, he exclaimed that American Vietnamese Catholics were "a gift from God" to his ministry.

He later wrote to me about his invalid nephew, who had been in a refugee camp in Thailand for eight years before being repatriated to Vietnam. He asked me to try to help him come to the U.S. Fortunately, my brother-in-law knew a Viet Kieu Roman Catholic priest in the Seattle area who appealed to his congregation and eventually arranged for the young man to come to the U.S.

Father Phuc and his seminarians (Hue, 2002)

Amazingly, the priest had a connection with Khe Sanh as well. In 1998, he wrote to tell me:

> Last Sunday, I have received in my church a group of ancient soldiers who [fought] in Vietnam, they [went] to Khe Sanh base where the fight was very dangerous. While I spoke [to] the visitors, an old soldier who was in Phu Bai camp: [said] Father Joseph, We remember you, when I was a soldier in Phu Bai camp, you brought your boys and girls to sing Christmas Carols. . . . Because for [my] priest's heart, as I used to say: For me, VC and GI are our Lord's sons. And many visitors [shook] my hands very strongly.

The priest maintained a seminary in his church for several years, and he had his twenty-five boys sing to me on my last visit. He nurtured a tenuous relationship with the Cong An as well. He told me that they came to his church to wish him Merry Christmas on Christmas Eve. Afterward, he slipped out of his house to minister to his far-flung congregation.

He also directed me to a Roman Catholic orphanage caring for children suffering the long-term effects of Agent Orange, a visit that changed my life forever.

Nevertheless, many Catholic prelates remained extremely reluctant to open up to foreigners. One nun in 1997 refused to give me her name, while another in 2002 whispered during our conversation and made me promise never to divulge her identity. Interestingly, one of my Vietnamese guides, whom I suspected had Communist connections, assured me that all Catholic priests were CIA.

Son My

Yet, the pain of war still resonated deeply in many Vietnamese. In my History of the Vietnam War course, I often required students to give an oral report on some aspect of the conflict. Interestingly, more students reported on the My Lai massacre than any other topic. However, their interest transcended some morbid fascination with the worst American atrocity in recent memory; instead they genuinely wanted to understand what happened at My Lai.

Despite its ever-present hold on the American psyche, I wondered how the Vietnamese felt about the atrocities and, more importantly, how they interpreted the events there. Twice in the summer of 2003, I traveled to Quang Ngai province in central Vietnam to visit the Son My memorial. (My Lai was part of cluster of villages called Son My. Because the killing occurred in more than one village, the Vietnamese commemorate the slaughter under the larger label of Son My.) Unsure of what to expect, I learned to my great surprise that the Vietnamese have turned the massacre site into an intensely moving memorial that projected solemnity, serenity, and conveyed a powerful call for peace. Indeed, many Vietnamese considered the violence that occurred at My Lai as a natural outgrowth of war and, thus, most expressed a deep desire to live in peace.

In the process, I encountered a community dedicated to preserving peace in order to avoid a repeat of My Lai. But I also stumbled upon four individuals who survived the ordeal and who still suffered deeply from war in one of its most horrific manifestations. Their experiences communicated important lessons about the value of peace during a time of seemingly perpetual conflict. The conversations also taught me that the My Lai survivors, like many American combat veterans, carried deep emotional scars that resided just beneath the surface ready to emerge at any time. Indeed, my interviews unlocked their horrendous memories as their stories burst forward in a blast of super-charged emotion that demonstrated to me once again the ghastly impact of violence and war on human beings. As a combat veteran, I found their responses at once familiar and profoundly disturbing.

On March 16, 1968, American soldiers entered a series of hamlets in central Vietnam commonly referred to as My Lai and, in a four-hour orgy of violence, rape and rage, executed over five hundred mostly elderly Vietnamese along with their children and grandchildren. For many Americans, My Lai remained a metaphor for an unpopular, perplexing, brutal conflict that most would just as soon forget. For the U.S. military, My Lai represented much more, given that it stood as a stain on the honor of the U.S. armed forces and also exerted an enormous influence on American commanders who genuinely feared a repeat of the dreadful incident that occurred there. On a more reflective level, My Lai and its aftermath provided us with an enduring and stunning message about the impact of combat and violence on human beings that reminded us of the terrible consequences and moral dilemmas that arise during wartime.

Aside from a large memorial in the center of the former village, most of the site featured numerous grave markers that

Son My grave markers (2003)

listed the names of dead family members. I found it shocking to read the grave stones and realize that, in many cases, grandparents, parents, and children perished in a mere four hours of savagery. For instance, one marker commemorated a family wherein the grandparents (ages 70 and 65), the parents (ages 42 and 34), and the children (ages 13, 9 and 1) had all died. Like most East Asians, the Vietnamese worship their ancestors. Hence, the complete destruction of three generations of a family represented an incalculable loss to the larger family and the community. As an American veteran, I felt deeply ashamed and embarrassed over the actions of my countrymen. Appalled by what I had witnessed, I found some solace in the fact that I worked for peace in the hope that we will never have another My Lai.

Nevertheless, the Vietnamese attempted to provide an even-handed assessment of the Americans. In fact, the Son My interpretive center displayed photos of some of the soldiers who carried out the massacre, but also the picture of an American serviceman who shot himself in the foot rather than take part in the killing. It also portrayed the U.S. Army decoration later presented to Hugh Thompson, who landed his helicopter in the midst of the slaughter and attempted to halt the butchery and evacuate some of the wounded. The center also had the names of the 504 Vietnamese who died at Son My listed on a black background that seems eerily reminiscent of the black granite Vietnam Veterans Memorial in Washington, D.C.

As I walked around, I spoke to a number of Vietnamese, including several busloads of children who had been brought to the site by their teachers. I asked the instructors what they hoped to

Son My memorial (2003)

accomplish by bringing children to Son My. All said that they wanted young people to understand the malevolent nature of warfare and to value a Vietnam that today lives in peace. Interestingly, most went out of their way to point out that they did not hate Americans; instead they believed that "something went wrong with the soldiers' minds that day." They generally viewed the incident as a reminder of the horrors of warfare and a statement about the need for peace in the world.

I felt deeply moved by the whole event and sought to find out if any survivors might be interested in talking to me about their experiences. Discovering that perhaps six still lived, I returned to Son My two weeks later to speak with them. As it turned out, the director of the Son My memorial, Pham Thanh Cong, was eleven years old on the day the Americans attacked the village. He told me that while the Americans had often burned parts of settlements, before that day they had never engaged in wholesale murder. Although he escaped and hid in a rice paddy until the killing ended, his whole family perished and he had no idea what happened to their bodies. During the attack, he could not imagine what was occurring and afterwards could never understand why his family had been destroyed. He told me that he feared war very much because he worried about what would happen to children during wartime. He had worked at the memorial since 1992 to fulfill his desire to remember and honor his family and to remind people about the depravity of war.

I assumed that, like many American combat veterans, he suffered from Post Traumatic Stress Disorder (PTSD). He disclosed that he often dreamt about that day and constantly wondered about the motivations of the U.S. soldiers. This theme arose in almost all of my conversations as many Vietnamese expressed bewilderment over the actions of the Americans. I admitted to Cong that I served in Vietnam at the time that the massacre transpired, but like him, I could not provide an adequate explanation for the murder of hundreds of innocent civilians. It occurred to me as he spoke that the few people who emerged alive suffered especially bitter loneliness, having lost all of their loved ones, never to see them again. In fact, as he recalled that terrible day, he spoke very slowly and profoundly to the point that I could understand much of what he said even with my limited Vietnamese. For me, the conversation represented an incredibly poignant experience, and I apologized for the actions of my fellow Americans, although I wondered if that meant much after his immeasurable loss.

Pham Thanh Cong, Son My (2003)

When I told him that I belonged to an American peace group and I wanted to use My Lai to help my students understand the importance of avoiding war, he thanked me with genuine affection and respect. Unexpectedly, he asked me if I would like to speak to other survivors. A few minutes later, I found myself sitting across the table from three elderly Vietnamese who witnessed parts of the massacre. Cong introduced me as a professor who worked for peace and taught American students about the evils of war. With that assurance, they consented to speak to me.

The tenor of these interviews differed dramatically from the earlier one. As soon as the first woman, Ha Thi Quyet, began to verbalize her experiences, an electrical current seemed to pulsate through the air and a tension-charged atmosphere seized the room. As she spoke, she kept pointing to the sky, describing the helicopters as they brought in the Americans. The other woman, Pham Thi Thuan, covered her face with her hands, while the man, Pham Dat, stared blankly into space. It seemed obvious that their memories of the tragedy remained fresh and extraordinarily painful as they reacted viscerally to my request that they recount their actions on that day.

According to Quyet, she was forty-eight years old at the time and only survived by hiding in an adjacent rice field. Wounded in the hip, she could not walk afterwards and relied on the compassion of local villagers to sustain her. She claimed that she received no assistance from the South Vietnamese government and lost nine family members. In fact, only the Viet Cong provided medical aid to the villagers, an action which no doubt led more of the local people to support the insurgency. Meanwhile, she harbored great sadness and anger about the conflict and only wanted peace, not war. As she finished her story, her voice trailed away as if she did not want to get to the terrible ending and the realization that her family had vanished forever.

Seething with anger as she told her story, Thuan was far more animated than the other interviewees. Thirty years old on the day of the attack, she also had been shot and only survived by lying under a pile of corpses, sheltering her baby as American soldiers continued to fire into the ditch. Someone later found her and nursed her back to health but, even so, she lost six family members during the attack.

Dat spoke last. In his mid-thirties when the assault occurred, he lost eleven family members and survived by hiding in his house. As he spoke, he pointed to the many different parts of his body where he had been shot. Suddenly, he became very agitated, and everyone in the room began to cry.

Son My survivors (2003)

It was the saddest, most heartbreaking moment I had ever witnessed. Dat told me that he felt terrified that day and has remained afraid of war ever since. In fact, he said that when the recent U.S. war with Iraq started, he felt compelled to watch TV all the time to observe the unfolding conflict because he had a feeling of impending doom, that a new war could somehow spark another cataclysm like Son My at any time.

When I asked how they felt about Americans, Thuan replied "our government wants to improve relations with the US," which was her way of telling me that the VCP would not permit her to express the hatred she felt for the Americans who carried out the atrocity. Quyet admitted that she remained very angry with the U.S. soldiers for years, but now she hoped for better cooperation between the U.S. and Vietnam and wanted Washington to start no more wars. Quyet also wanted vets like me to teach young people about the horrors of war. Dat asked me why the U.S. goes to war so often, but I could not really give him a satisfactory answer.

Astonishingly, despite the anger and hatred they felt towards the people who destroyed their families and their lives, they retained the ability to discern between the soldiers who killed their families and Americans in general. I found this really fascinating because I believe that racism—which often negates a person's individuality—stood behind the massacre. In other words, American racism towards the Vietnamese had been answered with an effort to distinguish between the actions of a few and Americans in general. All four people acknowledged that many individual Americans, mostly vets, have returned to Vietnam to try to help the Vietnamese people.

At this point, I terminated the interview, because I sensed how excruciating the process had become for them and had no desire to inflict any more pain. Yet, at the end, each person emotionally and sincerely thanked me for trying to tell the truth about war. I realized that, to them, the cause of the My Lai tragedy lay not with the Americans or the Viet Cong; the true culprit was and is war, because it forced people to live in a world of violence that over time led to greater brutality, dehumanization, and atrocity. Their horrific four hours taught them the universal truth that all war is hideous and that there are no good wars.

I already knew that after Khe Sanh, but nothing could have prepared me for the horrors I encountered that summer in the lovely, peaceful city of Hue.

The Orange-Colored Poison

"It's much worse in the countryside."
- Thich Nu Minh Tanh

While watching television one day during the 2004 presidential election, I noted a faintly familiar face on the screen among a group of Vietnam veterans criticizing Democrat John Kerry for his antiwar activities during the conflict. The program identified the speaker as a former Marine named Zumwalt who had served in the Vietnam War. Given his famous name, I instantly recalled a bizarre encounter we experienced in a strange venue in 1996.

That year, on my first return trip to Vietnam, I had stopped at the American War Crimes Museum in Ho Chi Minh City. Although the Vietnamese later renamed it the American War Remnants Museum in an act of international political correctness, the expositions of horribly wounded and mutilated Vietnamese civilians caused by U.S. bombing and atrocities left me depressed and consumed with self-reproach. Yet, those exhibits could not compare to the horrors of the Agent Orange section of the museum, which contained graphic photos of American and Vietnamese children suffering from the effects of defoliants. Equally arresting were the jars full of deformed babies born to mothers after the war.

On the wall in the Agent Orange room hung a photograph of Elmo Zumwalt, Jr. The former admiral and U.S. Chief of Naval Operations had dramatically raised American awareness of the long-term effects of defoliants by publishing an extraordinary book about his decision to spray chemicals in South Vietnam and the subsequent death of his son, a naval officer who served in Vietnam, from cancer most likely caused by Agent Orange. Zumwalt later exerted a critical influence on the Clinton administration by persuading it to treat veterans suffering from various ailments linked to Agent Orange. As I stood in front of his picture contemplating all of this, an American walked into the room with a Vietnamese who pointed to the photo of Zumwalt. I immediately launched into a long explanation about the admiral and his great work on behalf of vets. When I finished the man turned to me and said, "I know. He is my father." The younger Zumwalt had returned to honor his deceased brother's birthday.

Yet, for all of the emotion of that moment, even more graphic evidence greeted me on the streets of Ho Chi Minh City, where I encountered scores of children suffering from physical and mental deformities almost assuredly brought on by Agent Orange. One little girl especially brought this home to me. I often ate breakfast at an all-night restaurant in the Pham Ngu Lao district of Ho Chi Minh City. The outdoor coffee shop usually contained an interesting cast of characters, including brooding vets, numerous drunk and high foreigners staying at the mini-hotels that dot the area, prostitutes, and assorted hustlers, but also lots of physically and mentally challenged children. The little girl sat at my table one morning years ago and asked for a handout. Having already experienced serious beggar fatigue after a few days in the city, I declined, but then I paid for her breakfast as we engaged in a half-English/half-Vietnamese conversation. I soon appreciated that her life had been severely impacted because of her critical physical disabilities. Interestingly, every year when I returned, she would still be hanging around trying to hustle a few dollars. When I visited the same area in 2005, she had grown into adolescence while still wandering the streets. I told my wife that I had witnessed that little girl growing up on the boulevards of Saigon. In 2006, a Westerner told me that she had become a prostitute.

All the while, evidence piled up in various venues that a connection between the sick children of Vietnam and Agent Orange existed, despite persistent American government claims that no link could be established scientifically. Between 1962 and 1971, the U.S. sprayed some twenty million gallons of herbicides (generally referred to as Agent Orange because the containers holding the chemicals usually had an orange stripe around them) on Vietnam in an effort to deny forest cover and food to members of the insurgency. Ironically, most of the spraying took place over South

Vietnam, one of America's closest allies. Hence, in the twenty-first century, America's former friends in Vietnam witnessed the outrageous spectacle of seeing their grandchildren's lives destroyed by a weapon the U.S. deployed over four decades ago.

Some scientists argued that exposure to these agents contributed to high levels of skin diseases, respiratory ailments, immune-system disorders, neurological problems, and numerous forms of cancer in war veterans and their offspring. Moreover, the Vietnamese endured a long-term battering from defoliants, given that their explosive population growth in recent years demanded more land under cultivation, leading some scientists to conclude that farmers had unknowingly introduced long-dormant herbicides into the ecosystem, creating a new environmental onslaught against Vietnam. The large number of children with severe neurological problems coming into the world in 2005—thirty years after the war's conclusion—constituted the most troubling aspect of the new American chemical offensive.

While many historians had documented the gruesome record of U.S. efforts to eradicate Vietnamese Communism, far fewer had examined the war's bitter and long-term legacy on the innocents of Vietnam. Close to three million Vietnamese died, millions more suffered wounds, and over three hundred thousand remain listed as missing in action. The country experienced extensive infrastructure damage from the prolonged American bombing campaign and significant climatic change from the massive destruction of trees caused by American firepower.

Added to this depressing list of human tragedy was the ongoing plight of Amerasians left in Vietnam after the war, the unresolved fate of some of the boat people who fled the country, and the extreme poverty of Vietnam after 1975, partly caused by the ruinous American embargo against its former enemy. Yet, the massive ecological attack carried out against the Vietnamese people in the form of chemical defoliants represented the most egregious American wartime action and an undertaking for which the U.S. never acknowledged much responsibility. Nor did Washington attempt to correct the appalling human cost of its irresponsible actions during the war.

The presence of defoliants in the Vietnamese ecosystem created enormous trepidation in postwar Vietnam. Tragically, in a society that scorned and pitied childless women, some chose to remain childless rather than risk the consequences of Agent Orange. Others had multiple children in the hope that at least a few would be born healthy. The Vietnamese press added to the apprehension by running almost daily stories about the plight of families attempting to care for afflicted children.

Indeed, when I asked one Vietnamese woman how people in Vietnam felt about Agent Orange after the war, she responded immediately, "They were afraid." Thus, along with the significant physical and emotional damage brought on by the fighting, the Vietnamese particularly dreaded the effects of the ecological time bomb planted in their midst that still attacked their people, predominantly young people, generations after the war had ended. By 2006, the Vietnamese government estimated that over three hundred thousand children had been born with birth defects since the end of the war, and over a million Vietnamese had physical disorders brought on by Agent Orange. Many Vietnamese simply referred to Agent Orange as the Orange-Colored Poison.

After extreme pressure from the U.S. Congress, the Veterans Administration had finally recognized a number of Agent Orange-related ailments among American veterans. Yet, Washington steadfastly declined to provide compensation or effective relief to Vietnamese who had been diagnosed with the same conditions. Recently, a group of Vietnamese sued, in a U.S. court, the American chemical companies that had produced the herbicides, but a federal judge threw out their claim in March 2005, inciting a vigorous and outraged torrent of editorial opinion in the Vietnamese press.

Many allied and Communist soldiers also suffered exposure to these agents, which generated an astonishing commonality of health problems in Australian, South Korean, Vietnamese, and American veterans. However, the people of Vietnam paid an even more ghastly price since the agents remained in their environment. Unlike the foreigners who invaded their nation, most Vietnamese lacked the ability to flee from the long-term impact of the defoliants. Hence, it is in Vietnam that any effective long-term study of the impact of Agent Orange must take place.

Dioxin, an extremely toxic cancer-causing agent, was the deadliest by-product of Agent Orange. Moreover, recent research has demonstrated that the defoliants used during the conflict contained twice the amount of dioxin commonly believed in the years immediately after the war. When Washington discovered in

Agent Orange haunts third generation

Sorrow and joy: A doctor looks on as Agent Orange victims in Hà Nội's Peace village find a bit of time to relax. The village was setup about ten years ago as a place of refuge for victims of Agent Orange. — VNA/VNS Photo Dương Ngọc

HÀ TÂY — A 19-year-old with the build of a 10 year-old, Hồng Hạnh's body is "falling to pieces."

The victim of the most toxic defoliant known to man, her story is almost commonplace among the generations of children growing up in the Agent Orange wastelands of southern Việt Nam.

Hạnh was born 10 years after Agent Orange – containing the chemical dioxin – was sprayed during the prolonged American military campaign. And while her touching story made the front page of The Guardian newspaper's weekend section in March, she is just one of the chemical's estimated one million victims.

Repeated reports detailing the tortuous medical and environmental aftermath of Agent Orange have done little to evoke aid or redress from the nation that 30 years ago blanketed 2.8 million people with dioxin.

Now health authorities worry that a third generation of victims may fall further into oblivion, ineligible to receive already limited government aid.

In February of this year, the Government signed a mandate to provide financial support for Agent Orange victims. But its limited budget cannot cope with all their demands.

The director of the Fund for Agent Orange Victims, Lê Kế Sơn, said only soldiers and their children are subject to the aid.

"The main concern now is that victims of Agent Orange are not just soldiers and their children," he noted.

"It is a matter of genes, so the third generation of offspring from these soldiers is possibly infected," Sơn said.

"The State cannot cover all things," Minister of Labour, Invalids and Social Affairs Nguyễn Thị Hằng said.

The consequences of the chemical war brought to Việt Nam exceed the soothing power of money and time – it is extremely difficult to decontaminate soil and humans affected by dioxin, according to experts.

A World Health Organi-

National Academy of Science in 1974 – and that the 340kg of dioxin sprayed was double the quantity that had previously been disclosed.

The report also said that people in more than 20,585 hamlets were suffering from an array of baffling chronic conditions and that 2 to 4.8 million people may have been present during the aerial spraying of Agent Orange.

Nearly one-third of southern Việt Nam was razed by the chemical. Washed by rain into valleys, wells and ponds, the TCCD in Agent Orange polluted drinking water in much of the south.

One of the only large-scale projects for Agent Orange victims was set up in 1998 by the Red Cross of Việt Nam, having provided VND40 billion (US$2.6 million) in medical check-ups, orthopaedic operations and physical rehabilitation for 200,000 patients.

The President of the Việt Nam Red Cross Association, Nguyễn Trọng Nhân, said it was hard work to dissolve the consequences of war.

"We need more help from individuals as well as charities," he said.

"The US should assume responsibility for compensating the victims of the war."— VNS

sation briefing paper warns, "Once the TCCD [a strain of dioxin in Agent Orange] has entered the body it is there to stay due to its uncanny ability to dissolve in fats and to its rock solid chemical stability."

In April, American scientists announced that the amount of Agent Orange sprayed by US soldiers during the war totalled 100 million litres – not the 72 million litres claimed by the US

Quảng Ngãi works against big drought

QUẢNG NGÃI — The central province of Quảng Ngãi will spend VND13.2 billion (US$857,000) on dredging canals and increasing water supplies in drought-hit areas, the provincial People's Committee has announced. During this dry season, the province will mobilise 36,000 workers for drought-preparedness work.

Disadvantaged get free lodging in testing times

LÂM ĐỒNG — More than 1,500 disadvantaged students sitting for this year's university entrance exams in the Tây Nguyên (Central Highlands) province of Lâm Đồng will receive free accommodation, announced the provincial Youth Union. About 60 union members will be assigned to welcome provincial test-takers to Đà Lạt.

The union is also working with private lodging houses to provide cheap rooms for students.

Đà Nẵng's daily water supplies contaminated

ĐÀ NẴNG — Water for daily use in most of Đà Nẵng's wells is contaminated, said Trần Văn Nhật, director of the city's Preventive Medicines Department.

The announcement was made after the department tested water samples in four districts.

Lâm Đồng p...

Viet Nam News (2003)

the 1980s that a contractor had inadvertently sprayed dioxin onto a road in an American town a decade earlier, the U.S. government evacuated the community and sent in teams in full protective gear to attempt to clean up the problem. Yet, the same government that moved so determinedly in Missouri never acknowledged responsibility for the use of dioxin in Vietnam. Ironically, one department of the U.S. administration, the Environmental Protection Agency (EPA), believed that dioxin represented a major health risk to those who suffered even a minimal exposure to the agent, while another branch of the same government, the Veterans Administration (VA), steadfastly denied any link between dioxin and health problems in veterans.

For American veterans, the effort to gain recognition and compensation for their suffering was a long and grueling struggle. A federal statute that prohibited them from suing the U.S. government for its wartime actions seemed particularly infuriating to many vets. At one point, the VA's scandalous record in refusing to treat veterans afflicted with Agent Orange-related health problems appeared so bad that the U.S. Congress took responsibility for the issue away from the VA and assigned it to the Centers for Disease

Control (CDC). Unfortunately, the AIDS epidemic ensured that the CDC would soon hand it back to the VA, which continued to stall and temporize in identifying the problem. In fact, some commentators speculated that the U.S. government deliberately delayed a full-scale investigation of the impact of Agent Orange when physical difficulties among veterans first materialized, in the hope that many of the victims would die and take the fatal evidence of government treachery to their graves. The presence of other factors that could influence their health, such as smoking and drinking alcohol, and the fact that the U.S. government transferred the herbicides to the South Vietnamese government during the war complicated the issue for veterans. Thus, even though American pilots and aircraft sprayed almost all of the chemicals, technically the herbicides belonged to South Vietnam, an entity that no longer existed after 1975.

Eventually, a group of veterans sued the chemical companies that had produced the defoliants and won a settlement in 1984 of $180 million. Later, many veterans realized that the monetary award remained inadequate to meet their enormous medical needs. Finally, after extreme pressure from the U.S. Congress, the VA acknowledged a number of Agent Orange-associated ailments (but not the connection to Agent Orange): non-Hodgkin's lymphoma, prostate cancer, Chloracne, soft tissue sarcoma, Hodgkin's disease, respiratory cancers, multiple myeloma, and peripheral neuropathy. Despite the VA's acceptance of these occurrences, the U.S. government consistently refused to compensate the people of Vietnam or Korean veterans of the hostilities who suffered from the same conditions.

When I requested an Agent Orange profile, VA health-care workers remained more interested in convincing me that no health risk could be linked to Agent Orange than in discovering if I had any significant physical problems. I had to wait months for an appointment, and the doctor who examined me would not answer my questions or communicate with me in any meaningful way. At one point during the physical, VA employees required me to view a video that claimed no evidence existed that Agent Orange caused health problems, a statement that flew in the face of a substantial body of opinion and the VA's own acknowledgment of Agent Orange-linked diseases.

The terrible blight of Agent Orange afflicted others besides Americans and Vietnamese. When I taught in South Korea in 1998-

99, I discovered that a group of Korean veterans had demanded that the U.S. provide them with compensation for substantial troubles that they had incurred due to their exposure to Agent Orange. Their lawyer wanted to bring the issue to the United Nations (UN) or charge the U.S. with war crimes before the World Court for what, he argued, amounted to an American deployment of chemical weapons during the hostilities. Unfortunately, the U.S. appeared just as reluctant to provide justice to Korean veterans as it was to the people of Vietnam, which seemed unsurprising given Washington's history on the issue.

The School of the Beloved

Of course, the malevolent legacy of Agent Orange most deeply haunted the Vietnamese. Although I had observed many children with serious physical and mental abnormalities during my trips to Vietnam, it was not until December 2002 that I finally mustered the courage to confront the issue head-on and associate a human face with the scientific evidence. That month, I stopped at two privately run facilities in Hue that assisted children suffering from Agent Orange-related disabilities. At a Catholic orphanage that also oper-ated as a treatment center for thirteen children suffering from severe neurological disorders, I was surprised when a little boy in a high chair started eating his breakfast and all of the nuns began clapping.

But I understood why after the director told me that it had taken them a year to teach the boy how to hold a spoon, while another child spent four years learning how to walk. I felt abso-lutely horrified when I witnessed those small broken lives first hand. Finally, overwhelmed with shame, I admitted to the nuns that I was an American and then I broke down and cried. Yet, they treated me with kindness and compassion and assured me that they would ask the children to pray for me.

Later that day, I visited a Buddhist treatment center called Thuy By (School of the Beloved) that had over fifty children suffer-ing from Agent Orange-associated ailments. One child remained so incapacitated that two staffers massaged her hands and feet so that she might gain some feeling in her extremities, while others gave individual attention to the more severe cases and held classes for other children. As I walked around, the director, Thich Nu Minh Tanh, pointed out that four of the children came from one family.

She also told me that while she attempted to help as many children as possible, the situation in the countryside, where most of the spraying occurred, remained far worse and few children there received any effective treatment. She claimed that almost all of her financial support came from private individuals. In fact, two Swiss and one American had built her facility with private funds and named it the School of the Beloved. I told the nun that I considered her a living Buddha for bringing so much compassion to those tormented children. Even so, she acknowledged that she felt great anger towards Americans for the misery they had caused so many children.

At the time, I could not determine what seemed worse, American ignorance or indifference over the fragile lives we continued to devastate. Nevertheless, I understood that our head-in-the-sand attitude and collective amnesia had damaged our international image and convinced many Vietnamese that our calls for Human Rights amounted to astonishing hypocrisy. For many years, the ostensible reason Washington had given for declining help to Vietnam had been the lingering suspicion that it still held American prisoners from the war. However, the U.S. military had arrived at plausible explanations for the fate of almost all of the men still listed as missing. Thus, it seemed obvious that political and financial considerations prevented Washington from assisting the Vietnamese and coming to terms with the impact of Agent Orange.

By this point, many Americans accepted the fact that the war had been a dreadful, tragic U.S. mistake. Yet, residual feelings of hostility towards the Vietnamese and the cynical manipulation of the families of the MIAs drove my country to deny aid to Vietnam in its quest to escape the ecological disaster placed on it by the U.S. Many observers had commented on the fact that the U.S. continued to suffer from a deep psychological malaise brought on by the war. However, Americans will probably never recover from Vietnam until they and their government take responsibility for U.S. actions during the war.

For me, the Agent Orange catastrophe had suddenly become very personal. That night, I e-mailed my wife and told her that I had just spent my worst day in Vietnam (I was wrong) and that for the first time, I had cried in Vietnam, not over what happened to us, but rather for what we did to its children. I wondered: What did they ever do to deserve this? They were not combatants. They were innocent children whose lives had been damaged by American weapons deployed in a conflict that ended decades ago. I questioned who would take responsibility for these shattered lives.

That afternoon became a life-changing experience as I realized that I had to attempt to undo some of the pain we had inflicted by reminding Americans of the appalling legacy of the war that I had witnessed in the children of Vietnam. As I fought my way through a firestorm of guilt, disbelief, and depression, I became determined to find a way to confront Agent Orange.

Thus, I embarked on an emotional, financial, and physical journey to lend a hand to the sick children of Vietnam and sustain the nun who had assured me that "here misery becomes action." I began financially supporting the nun and her enormous social welfare network while also utilizing my position as an academic to publicly call attention to the plight of the children. In my first public talk about the matter, at Berea College in Kentucky shortly after the George W. Bush administration attacked Iraq allegedly to seize its weapons of mass destruction, I identified Agent Orange as the "Ultimate Weapon of Mass Destruction: A Silent Killer that Destroys Future Generations."

In this and later presentations, I discovered that many Americans remained totally unaware of the crisis brought on by Agent Orange in Vietnam and few appreciated the Vietnamese government's limited financial and technical ability to confront the challenge. Sadly, for most Americans, Vietnam still represented a war rather than a place. I often pointed out that it seemed outrageous that a country that spent more on defense than the rest of the world combined could not spare any money for children sickened by America's obsession with winning wars through the application of science-driven military technology.

Indeed, I argued that one B-2 bomber cost over $2 billion and the new advanced strike fighter system came with a price tag of $200 billion. Yet, in contrast to our profligate spending in our frustrating and ultimately futile search for security in an insecure world, one billion dollars could change thousands of lives in Vietnam and convince many Vietnamese that we are a people capable of meting out justice as effectively as firepower.

Eventually, I decided to return to Hue that following summer and spend two months in and around the city with Thich Nu Minh Tanh examining the problem in much greater detail. On this and subsequent excursions, I encountered something unimaginable that changed my life and my perspective towards Vietnam forever. Nevertheless, amid the misery of rural Vietnam, the nun seemed undaunted in her efforts to bring compassion and succor to the poor, especially children suffering from Agent Orange. I soon learned that she had recently opened a vocational school to train disabled Vietnamese to earn a living in the new global economy, and that she also had an extensive outreach program in the countryside. In many ways, she was a one-person social welfare network ministering to the poor in Hue, the Highland people in the countryside, orphans, land-mine victims, rural kids, blind children, children with no clothes, adults suffering from the war, hospitalized youth and, always, children experiencing the impact of Agent Orange, both those attending her institution and others too sick, too poor, or too enfeebled to make it to her school.

The nun built houses for people in the countryside, although it was difficult to get to the Highlands because of continuing government oppression of America's wartime allies. She estimated that it cost $400 to build one residence for twelve people. But she had helped over 700 individuals on the Buddha's birthday by providing them $10 each, although she preferred the long-term impact of erecting homes rather than the short-term benefit of handing people money. She pointed out that many central Vietnamese lived in bamboo huts throughout the rainy season, so she furnished them with blankets during the winter and mosquito nets in the summer.

As we began to work together, the nun enlightened me on her difficult relationship with the Communist Party. To open the School of the Beloved, she had to obtain government permission, which took two years. Then, on the day it opened, even though she had raised all of the money from private donors, local Communist Party officials showed up to take credit for its construction. She even offered me a black-and- white photo of the event to back up her assertion.

Thich Nu Minh Tanh also had a difficult time with the Cong An (the Communist Police) and had been forced to pay bribes on a regular basis to keep operating. On a later trip, she declared that the Communists had told her that they would not block her from emigrating if she wished, but the nun wanted to stay so that she could keep on assisting the sick children. Nevertheless, her ability to merge her religious ideology with hard-nosed business sense remained a source of constant surprise for me. At the same time, she worked hard to satisfy my desire for information about the Buddhist peace movement so that I could help the children.

The cleric also arranged for me to visit a large number of dwellings in the city and the surrounding area so that I could examine the impact of Agent Orange on the daily lives of the local residents. The night before I embarked on my first rural excursion, I had a terrible nightmare and woke myself up screaming.

My unsettled sleep served as a fitting prelude for the horrors I witnessed over the next few weeks as I encountered human anguish on a scale that dwarfed anything I had ever endured at Khe Sanh. Even worse, the victims were not the young, vigorous Marines I associated with the fighting, many of whom had the opportunity to rebuild their lives after the war. Instead, they were broken, crippled, helpless children brought low by a weapon that my country had launched against their grandparents. I feared, then and now, that I lacked the resources to adequately describe the nightmarish existence we created in Vietnam with Agent Orange.

VCP officials celebrate school opening (Thuy By)

The next day, we visited a number of homes inhabited by invalid children, many of whom stayed home all day by themselves. Numerous homes had thatched roofs with no furniture and little cover for the children from the elements. That situation, combined with their lack of mobility, made for unspeakable living conditions. Most homes contained more than one sick child afflicted by what the Vietnamese euphemistically referred to as "nervous problems." At one home, as we walked up to the door, a thirteen-year-old child flopped across the floor like a fish to greet us. In a particularly adept display of her adroit public relations skills, the nun often had me hand the children an envelope of money along with other small gifts.

Thich Nu Minh Tanh handing out gifts (Hue, 2003)

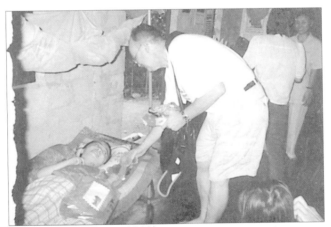

Bedridden child (Hue, 2003)

As we moved from one hovel to another, I attempted to steel myself for the inevitable shock on the other side of the next doorway. All the while, I could not flee from the knowledge that my country had inflicted this pain on these parents and children.

At one home, which consisted of one room with a leaky roof, a woman and her other three children lived with a fifteen-year-old boy who had been bedridden his whole life.

He could not sit or stand but seemed like a sweet lad, although I wondered at the awfulness of spending every waking moment in such a dreadful environment. After the father died, the mother shouldered the burden of raising four children by herself while ministering to the severely disabled boy. At one point, he said "I put my refuge in the Buddha" and the nuns all started to cry, but the mother had wept from the moment we walked through the door. Many of the mothers told us that they wanted to send their sick offspring to school but could not afford the transportation, or their children remained too disabled to attend. In fact, the nun ministered to over 240 children in the area who were experiencing Agent Orange ailments. I recoiled from the thought of living in those small homes day after day with children suffering from such severe disabilities.

Conditions in the next house appeared even more unspeakable. A thirteen-year-old girl lived in a dwelling that had about an inch of water on the floor with ducks wandering around inside and a working fire in the back. The heat in the house was absolutely oppressive, and I could not understand how anyone could live in such an unhealthy environment. The nun told me that the family had four children, two of whom had developed neurological illnesses. The little girl we had come to visit could not sit up by herself, and when her mother left her for a second she fell backwards and her tiny head crashed into the cement floor. The nun let me know that she loved her so much and wanted to see her go to school.

Later, we entered a home in the Catholic Phu Cam district of Hue, where a severely disabled fourteen-year-old-boy lived alone and received minimal amounts of care from a cousin who also had a neurological disability. The house consisted of a bed and nothing more except for four walls and a roof. I wondered why the nun brought me there, but then I realized that she wanted to demonstrate the ecumenical nature of her ministry. In her view, even Catholics deserved compassion.

Sick boy in Phu Cam (2003)

That evening, I spent another terrible night. This had only been the first of many days investigating the impact of Agent Orange. Nevertheless, the nun cautioned me that I had to remember "It's much worse in the countryside." When I arrived back at her pagoda the next morning, Thich Nu Minh Tanh said I looked thinner after only two days. She told me that her American benefactor had cut her off because he wanted to have better relations with the Vietnamese government, which remained highly suspicious of social outreach activities by Buddhists, particularly the nun who had previously belonged to the banned Unified Buddhist Church (UBC).

A few days later, the children at the School of the Beloved held a party for me at which I met most of the staff. Buying candy for the children that morning became a community activity, as everyone in the store and on the sidewalk discussed the proper food/gifts for the kids. I found over fifty children waiting for me at the school, because they knew that I was bringing snacks and drinks. When I arrived, they stood up and tried collectively to say "hello" and then "thank you" to me. They also struggled to sing a song, but some stood up while others sat down in a confused and chaotic attempt to follow their teachers' instructions. Overall, it seemed extraordinarily touching and dreadful at the same time. Like most disabled children they craved physical contact. Many of them hugged the nun when she walked through the door, and most tried to hold my hand, embrace me, or make some kind of contact. When I returned to the school in 2005, a little girl ran up and gave me a hug as soon as I walked through the door. As I left, I heard the nun telling the father of one of the children that the parents might have to pay to keep the school open if she could not find a financial donor.

I also gained much more information about the financial structure of the school. The nun employed seventeen people overall, including two occupational therapists, two cooks, one guard, one accountant, several teachers, and one janitor. In addition, she sometimes paid a doctor to come to the school to check on the children. Each employee earned 500,000 dong ($33) a month, plus the nun paid 100,000 dong ($6) a month for health insurance for each of her employees.

All of the employees gave back part of their salaries to help the children. Thus, her total monthly salary expense came to 8,500,000 dong ($566). By the time I left Hue, I had changed my

Thuy By party (Hue, 2003)

Thuy By Teachers (Hue, 2003)

mind and agreed to support the school completely for a year. That day, I gave the teachers 500,000 dong, which they decided to split evenly among themselves, which was so typical of the communal sprit of Vietnam.

On the same trip, as I became overwhelmed with remorse over the actions of my government and the continuing impact of the war on the Vietnamese, I ran into several individuals in Hue who provided me with a different perspective. One morning, as I drank coffee at an outdoor café in Hue, I heard someone speaking American-style English. I discovered to my delight that he was an ex-Marine, a Khe Sanh veteran, and a water engineer from California who had come to Vietnam to build water systems on his own time for the Vietnamese. His friend, a former Navy Seal, would not tell me what he did during the war, which was fine, because I did not really want to know. More importantly, both vets had returned to Vietnam to help the Vietnamese. In fact, they had purchased a ton of rice and given it to a Vietnamese village and also had donated sewing machines to disabled Vietnamese in order for them to learn a new craft. Indeed, individual Americans were trying to do something about the problems brought on by the war.

Gio Linh

A few days afterward, the nun took me to a school/clinic for disabled children in Gio Linh only fourteen kilometers from the Ben Hai River, the old border between North and South Vietnam. Gio Linh had been the northernmost hamlet in the former South Vietnam. The driver of our van seemed very nervous, mainly because we lacked a travel pass to go into the old DMZ area. I constantly assured him that I sought no trouble with the Cong An and that we only wanted to do good work.

At the School for Disabled Children Suffering from Agent Orange in Gio Linh, I discovered a center that attempted to assist 127 sick children. The moment I stepped out of the car, I entered upon human misery on a scale that I would have never believed possible as I viewed scores of mentally and physically disabled children living in conditions that Charles Dickens would have considered shocking. Many were blind and/or deaf, some had lost their memories, and others appeared horribly deformed. The school/clinic had no doctor but employed three nurses who expressed outrage over the refusal of the U.S. to come to the aid of the sick children of Vietnam. The nurses earned only 200,000 dong

($13) a month, but each gave back a fourth of his/her salary to the clinic to support the children.

My presence generated lots of excitement, particularly when the nun told the assembled multitude that a giao su (professor) from the United States had come to their school to present gifts to the children. Before dispensing the aid, the nun led the children in prayer and made them promise they would try their best to study and learn even though they had disabilities, because the most important thing was for them to become good people.

The nun again demonstrated her sharp public skills as she instructed the children to express gratitude to me for my kindness. Then a Vietnamese man (perhaps a local party official) thanked us on behalf of the parents and expressed the desire that no more disabled children would come into the world. As she started to hand out the aid, the nun told everyone that we understood the pain of the children, so we had brought help including some dry noodles and a little cash (100,000 dong or $6) for each child.

Children praying (Gio Linh (2003)

Eventually, many of the desperately poor central Vietnamese overcame their shyness, and a procession of parents approached to ask me to help their children. One man came back three times and pleaded with me to assist his daughter. It was both unspeakable and unnerving to witness such agony in an area in close proximity to the DMZ that I knew had been saturated with Agent Orange during the fighting. Many tried to ease my obvious distress by

Gio Linh Nurses (2003)

assuring me that they did not blame individual Americans for the plight of the children but instead saw it as a problem between our governments. As my translator Han pointed out, "Many people here only see the pain. They don't really understand the reason. Everyone hopes for effective treatment but only the government can do it."

Days later, we visited a deserted village in Phu Bai, south of Hue. Only three people still lived there: a sister and her two brothers. All three suffered from severe disabilities. The nun told me that one man had been fine until he reached his mid-thirties and then suddenly lost the use of his legs. I was absolutely shocked as I watched the sister, who seemed far healthier than the other two, attempt to drag her brother from one area to another. Apparently everyone else had fled the rural community, because virtually every villager who tarried had developed serious illnesses.

My translator speculated that perhaps the water supply that served the community had been poisoned, but I thought I had figured it out already. Earlier as we drove down the highway toward the rural community, we passed a number of old American bunkers that had been part of the perimeter of our former base at Phu Bai. Thus, the village sat at the edge of what had been an American outpost. Often during the war, American forces sprayed extra Agent Orange around their perimeters to open up more effective fields of fire. This could have been especially true at Phu Bai, where local insurgents often probed our lines at night. Hence, the villagers may have become ill because of the residual dioxin in

Phu Bai (2003)

their soil and water left over from our spraying. Phu Bai had been my last duty station before I rotated out of Vietnam in 1968 so, in a weird kind of way, I had a connection to the base that may still have been carrying out a sustained assault against the local villagers.

I spent weeks traveling through a seemingly lush countryside full of human beings devastated by Agent Orange. But, as we drove down Highway Nine on the way back to Hue from Lao Bao, I suddenly spotted Hill 1015, the high point overlooking Khe Sanh. The nun must have appreciated my strong feelings about the battle. She asked if I wanted to stop at my old base, the place that had resided so firmly in my consciousness and had ruled so much of my life as it compellingly repelled and attracted me over the intervening decades.

To my great surprise, I said no, because I had more vital things to do. The sick children of Vietnam suddenly seemed much more important than my war. Their fight for justice had become my battle, and I was determined to win this time.

Conclusion

After eleven trips to Vietnam, I still found it impossible to come to terms with a conflict that caused such long-term damage to Americans and Vietnamese. Finally, it dawned on me that all of the arguments about the war, that "They wouldn't let us fight," and that we had to fight with one arm tied behind our back, had blocked us from the most important action: achieving reconciliation with the Vietnamese. The stark pain of war so readily apparent in Vietnam convinced me that the time had arrived to seek reconciliation with the Vietnamese. I came to believe that until we took responsibility for our actions in Vietnam, acknowledged the human misery that we caused, and then did something about it, Americans would never really achieve peace and would remain at war with each other over the conflict.

In many ways, confronting the unfinished business of war sparked a crisis of understanding for me that raised numerous unanswered questions as I attempted to negotiate my way through the human wasteland formerly called South Vietnam. I wondered: Why do people cling so tightly to memories of wartime loss? Do they have an innate need to believe that their sacrifices meant something? If Americans and South Vietnamese died and suffered for nothing during the war, does my life mean anything? What about the brave, young Marines who departed this existence while defending Khe Sanh? What did their sacrifices signify? Why have the former ARVN suffered so deeply? Was their resolve to fight based only on bad decisions on their part, assuming they had any input in the choice anyway? What real alternatives did they, or we, have? Was all of this foreordained so that we could return as better people in a later existence, or the unspeakable alternative? Can we accept that the war took place for naught and that the cynics who sat it out seem right and we appear more badly mistaken with each passing day?

My emotional and physical journey enabled me to locate a different Vietnam from the one I had known in 1968. In the process, I discovered a desperately poor land struggling to escape the ravages of decades of war followed by a ruinous American embargo designed to punish the Vietnamese for defeating us in a confrontation many Vietnamese never really wanted to fight. I also witnessed a level of human suffering left over from the war that remained inconceivable to most Americans. And for what? Today, the U.S. stands as Vietnam's number one trading partner, a privately owned coffee plantation operates on the old Khe Sanh battlefield, CitiBank owns one of the largest buildings in downtown Ho Chi Minh City, members of the Vietnamese Army train with the U.S. military, and President Bush visited Vietnam in 2006.

What a stunning revelation to recognize that I wasted years of rage, hatred, and resentment on a people who did not loathe me in return. Over time, I recognized that I had far more in common with the people of Vietnam, on both sides, than with most of my fellow citizens. On each journey back to Vietnam, the people seemed infinitely more human and less threatening than I recalled. Several years ago, a Korean questioning the war asked me, "Why did you attack that little country?" I found myself raising the same question more and more as I confronted the baffling situation in a postwar Vietnam that seemed to admire everything American. I wondered who had received a heavier dose of indoctrination during the war, them or us?

I grasped that if every American could connect the Vietnamese with their humanity and put a human face on our former enemies, much of the hostility between us would fade. What a terrible catastrophe this had been: decades of bitterness and enmity between people who could have been friends. Yet, my excursions to Vietnam convinced me that most Vietnamese had forgiven us far more than we had absolved ourselves. My onetime enemies in Vietnam greeted me with open arms, former ARVN hailed me on the street everywhere in the south and recounted how much they still liked Americans, while war-loving chicken hawks in the U.S. launched repeated, shameful attacks on Vietnam vets.

Glossary of Terms

III MAF	Third Marine Amphibious Force, headquartered in Danang—responsible for I Corps.
ARVN	Army of Republic of South Vietnam, the South Vietnamese Army.
August Revolution	The successful seizure of power by the Ho Chi Minh led Viet Minh in August 1945.
Bru	Local Montagnard tribe who inhabited the area around Khe Sanh.
Cao Dai	Vietnamese religion founded in the 1920s and based on spiritism: eventually moved their headquarters to Tay Ninh, close to the border with Cambodia.
CAP	Combined Action Platoon, used extensively by the U.S. Marine Corps in an attempt to pacify the South Vietnamese countryside. Many Marines resided in the villages under this program.
Charlie Med	The main medical evacuation facility at Khe Sanh.
CincPac	Commander in Chief Pacifici commanded all U.S. forces in the Pacific; including Vietnam.
Cong An	The Communist police who exercised considerable authority inVietnam, widely known for their corruption and hostility

towards foreigners. As many as two-thirds of Cong An work undercover.

DMZ

Demilitarized Zone, the area separating North and South Vietnam.

DRV

Democratic Republic of Vietnam, better known as North Vietnam during the war.

Doi Moi

Revitalization or the new thinking a plan implemented by the VCP in an effort to introduce market forces into the Vietnamese economy.

Giac Ngo

(*Enlightenment*) A Buddhist magazine published in Ho Chi Minh City.

Hoa Hao Buddhism

A fundamentalist form of Buddhism found mostly in the Mekong Delta region of Vietnam. Founded in 1939 by Huynh Phu So.

Hospital Corpsmen

Navy personnel who served in a medical capacity.

I CORPS

The northernmost provinces of South Vietnam.

Indian Country

Any area outside of American lines.

MACV

Military Assistance Command Vietnam, the overall military command for all American forces in South Vietnam.

Montagnards

Indigenous people of Vietnam.

Neo-con

Neo-conservatives, a group of former left wingers who became ardent conservatives and believers that the U.S. should use its military power to transform the world.

NLF

National Liberation Front, usually called the Viet Cong, mostly made up of southern guerillas.

PAVN

Peoples Army of Vietnam, better known as the North Vietnamese Army.

PRC	Peoples Republic of China, often referred to as Red China during the Cold War.
PTSD	Post Traumatic Stress Disorder, a psychological illness resulting from stressful events; can be combat-related or the result of other trauma. Because of the unique circumstances of the Vietnam War, Vietnam veterans displayed an extremely high prevalence of PTSD.
RAS	Regimental Aid Station at Khe Sanh, medical facility located on the eastern end of the base, close to the ammo dump.
Trung Sisters	Two women who carried out a rebellion against the Chinese in the first century A.D., considered the great cultural and military heroes of Vietnam.
UBC	Unified Buddhist Church, founded in 1964 in an effort to bring peace to Vietnam, subsequently banned by the Communist Party after 1975.
UN	United Nations.
UXO	Unexploded ordinance.
VCP	Vietnamese Communist Party, ruled North Vietnam from 1954 to 1975 and has since held sway over reunified Vietnam.
VHD	Vien Hoa Dao, Institute for the Propagation of the Dharma, the political arm of the radical Buddhists in the 1960s.
Viet Kieu	Overseas Vietnamese, Vietnamese living outside of Vietnam.
Viet Minh	A revolutionary nationalist organization created by Ho Chi Minh during World War II with the intention of expelling France from Vietnam.